# CONVERSATIONS *with* GOD

PRAYERS FOR JEWISH WOMEN

# CONVERSATIONS *with* GOD

PRAYERS FOR JEWISH WOMEN

## RUCHI KOVAL

MOSAICA PRESS

Mosaica Press, Inc.
© 2016, 2022 by Mosaica Press
Designed and typeset by Daniella Kirsch

All rights reserved
ISBN-10: 1937887561
ISBN-13: 978-1-937887-56-8

No part of this publication may be translated, reproduced, stored in a retrieval system or transmitted in any form or by any means, electronic, mechanical, photocopying, recording, or otherwise, without prior permission in writing from both the copyright holder and the publisher.

Published and distributed by:
Mosaica Press, Inc.
www.mosaicapress.com
info@mosaicapress.com

*In loving memory of my father*

## Jerry Pollak

*Who spent practically his entire life as "Legendary Mensch" in his home filled with Jewish women, and was often Hashem's answer to our prayers*

לעילוי נשמת ישראל בן יוסף מאיר, ז״ל

*Rise and Shine,
Suzie Pollak Becker*

בס"ד

## Congregation Ahavas Yisroel
1700 South Taylor Road
Cleveland Heights, Ohio 44118
216-932-8725

**Horav Boruch Hirschfeld**
*Rabbi*
**Rabbi Moshe Berger**
*President*

2 Adar, 5774
March 2014

I read and was inspired by the deep words on Tefillah [prayer] written by Mrs. R. Koval. This is not just a translation or commentary, but also a "close to text" summary, with verbalization of the emotional feelings that should accompany each blessing.

Although it was initially composed as a tool to help those who are new to talking to Hashem, it can definitely help all of us increase the quality of our Tefillah.

Therefore I humbly suggest that both men and women read and incorporate these concepts when talking to Hashem.

Rabbi Boruch Hirshchfeld

Rabbi, Congregation Ahavas Yisroel
Rosh Kollel, Ateres Chaim Baruch
Cleveland Heights, Ohio

# Table of Contents

Foreword ............................................................................... 11
Acknowledgments ............................................................... 13
Introduction ......................................................................... 15
How to Use This Book ........................................................ 17
What This Book Is Not ....................................................... 19
The Order (Siddur) of Prayer Books ................................. 21

DAILY PRAYERS ................................................................ 23
Modeh Ani ........................................................................... 25
Asher Yatzar ........................................................................ 26
My Soul ................................................................................ 27
Torah Blessings ................................................................... 29
Morning Blessings .............................................................. 31
Baruch She-Amar ............................................................... 38
Ashrei ................................................................................... 40
Halleluyah ........................................................................... 44
Yishtabach ........................................................................... 46
Shema ................................................................................... 48

Mi Kamocha .................................................................................... 57
Tzur Yisrael..................................................................................... 58
Amidah ........................................................................................... 59
Torah Reading for Mondays, Thursdays, and Shabbat ....................... 80
Kaddish........................................................................................... 83
Alaynu............................................................................................. 86
Nighttime Shema ............................................................................ 89
Adon Olam ..................................................................................... 94

# GRATITUDE AFTER EATING............................................................99

# SHABBAT ........................................................................................ 115
Prayer on Challah Baking ............................................................. 117
Candlelighting for Shabbat and Holidays ..................................... 118
Shalom Aleichem........................................................................... 123
Aishet Chayil ................................................................................. 125
Kiddush.......................................................................................... 129
Handwashing................................................................................. 131
Hamotzi......................................................................................... 132
Shabbat Amidah ............................................................................ 133
Havdallah....................................................................................... 149

# VARIOUS PRAYERS ....................................................................... 153

# FAMILY............................................................................................ 155
To Find a Soulmate ....................................................................... 155
On One's Wedding Day ................................................................. 156
Mikveh Prayer ............................................................................... 157
A Woman's Prayer for Her Husband and for Their Marriage ........ 159

To Become Pregnant .................................................................. 160
During Pregnancy ..................................................................... 162
Husband's Prayer While Wife Is in Labor ............................... 163
After a Miscarriage or Stillbirth ............................................... 164
Parents' Prayer for Their Children .......................................... 165
Children's Prayer for Their Parents ........................................ 167
Sending Children Off to School ............................................... 168
For Raising Special Needs Children ........................................ 169
On Day of Child's Bar/Bat Mitzvah ......................................... 170
On Day of Child's Wedding ...................................................... 171
To Say at the Gravesite of a Loved One................................... 172

## ISRAEL AND SPIRITUALITY ................................................ 175

Welcoming Holidays .................................................................. 175
Safety for Israel and the Israeli Soldiers ................................. 176
Rosh Chodesh — a New Jewish Month .................................. 177
For Help on One's Spiritual Journey........................................ 178
At the Western Wall and Other Holy Sites ............................. 179

## OTHER VARIOUS PRAYERS ................................................... 180

When Hearing of a Tragedy ..................................................... 180
Prayer for Peace ......................................................................... 181
Aging with Grace ....................................................................... 182
Forgiveness ................................................................................. 185
For Self to Remain Healthy....................................................... 186
For Others Who Are Ill ............................................................. 187
To Speak Positively of Others................................................... 187
For Safe Travels .......................................................................... 189
After Having a Bad Dream........................................................ 190

*Table of Contents*   9

To Find Lost Objects ........................................................................ 191
Dealing with Suffering .................................................................... 192

## PSALMS ........................................................................................ 193
Psalm 23 .......................................................................................... 195
Psalm 30 .......................................................................................... 197
Psalm 100 ........................................................................................ 199
Psalm 121 ........................................................................................ 200
Psalm 130 ........................................................................................ 202

## CONCLUSION ............................................................................ 205
When God Says No ........................................................................ 207

## APPENDIX .................................................................................. 209
Recommended Reading ................................................................ 211
About the Author ............................................................................ 214
About Mosaica Press ...................................................................... 215
About the Cover .............................................................................. 216

# Foreword

## BY REBBETZIN FEIGE TWERSKI

Prayer in Jewish sources is referred to as "service of the heart." It is a medium provided by the Master of the World in His ultimate compassion to invite man to seek Him out, communicate with Him and thus forge a relationship with Him.

Our Sages have identified ten different varieties of prayer. Prayer can be both formal and informal. A mere plea of "Please God, let my child do well on her test" is considered a prayer. Whenever and whichever way we address our concerns, desires, and wants heavenward constitutes as prayer. Prayer is a venue that gifts man with the privilege of choosing the time and place to initiate an encounter with his Creator. In addition to an ongoing dialogue with God that one can invoke spontaneously, we have the structured prayers of morning (*Shacharis*), afternoon (*Minchah*), and evening (*Maariv*). The text of these prayers was formulated by the *Anshei K'nesses Hagedolah,* the Men of the Great Assembly, over two thousand years ago. This august body included prophets, Talmudic sages, judges, grammarians, and great poets. With Divine inspiration they chose every word, phrase, and sentence with great care and exactitude. Hence, there are layers upon layers of meaning hidden in the often inscrutable words of the liturgy. Of great consequence are the selections devoted to the praise of the Almighty. These verses of adulation are not intended to flatter God or placate Him. In His absolute perfection, the Almighty is not dependent upon man's acclaim. Rather, the liturgy is designed to instruct and inspire. Through the discerning sight of exalted souls who saw and knew what we cannot possibly apprehend fully, we learn to appreciate some of the majesty, glory, and grandeur of the Being to whom we address our prayers.

As we grow in our knowledge of the language of the Torah, its precepts, intimations, and nuances, we get deeper and deeper glimpses into words and concepts, the understanding of which heretofore eluded us. As we mature in our skills and insights and become more conversant with the intricacies of Torah thinking, our appreciation for the formal prayers expands. Hidden vistas of meaning open up for us and enrich our prayer experience. It should also be noted that these prayers have escorted us throughout the generations, for thousands of years. They are the very same supplications of our ancestors and the same prayers that, with minor variations, are embraced by Jews in all four corners of the world.

Unfathomable as they may appear, at the most basic level they present us with a most worthy and exalted vessel in which to pour the entreaties of our heart. They may be the same words for everyone, but the final offering to God is individual to every person. Moreover, at any given time or moment, the same person may invest the words with new and different thinking. Bottom line is that it is a "service of the heart" and every heart pulsates with its own unique rhythm. At the end of the day prayer is a very personal experience.

In this volume, Ruchi Koval has given us a wonderful and attainable point of departure, a springboard to the journey of a lifetime. Her warm and insightful rendering of the many formal and informal prayers give us a taste so delightful and substantive that it will surely spur its users to go further to excavate the richness that doesn't readily meet the eye.

Ruchi's work is accessible, uplifting, and enriching. Clearly it comes from a heart longing for connection and therefore is certain to resonate with all who make use of it.

May all of our prayers find favor in the heavenly spheres and may our heavenly Father bless each and every one of us with the best of everything.

# Acknowledgments

I thank Wendy Solganik, as this was all her idea.

I thank the Luscious Verde *mussar* group, for being her crucible to birth it.

I thank my husband, Rabbi Sruly Koval, for supporting this endeavor and every other that strikes my fancy.

I thank Mosaica Press, headed by Rabbi Yaacov Haber and Rabbi Doron Kornbluth, for believing in it, improving it immensely, and seeing a need for it.

I thank Allyson Goldstein, the designer, and Robin Green, for the creation of the cover.

I thank Rabbi Moshe Dovid Choueka, for expertly supplying all the Hebrew text that appears here.

I thank all those who have used its pages at JFX High Holidays and *bnei mitzvah* services; I thank Aish Detroit and Etz Chaim of Baltimore for requesting its use.

I thank two extremely busy spiritual mentors, Rebbetzin Feige Twerski and Aliza Bulow, for giving me the gift of their time and enhancing this work with many important suggestions.

I thank Jill Katz and Hallie Abrams for generously sponsoring this book.

I thank the women who lovingly created my Mussar Fund in honor of my 40th birthday, which made this book possible: Allison, Allyson,

Audrey, Avril, Beth, Bassy, Carrie, Cheryl, Chris, Cindi, Elana, Francine/Tzipi, Gena, Giela, Hallie, Jamie, Jenny, Jill, Jody, Judy, Julie, Karen, Kim, Laura, Lauren, Lisa, Loren, Malky, Yael, Marci, Nancy, Ranya, Robin, Chany and the Beachwood *mussar* class, Samantha, Shari, Shawna, Sherrie, Sindy, Sydney, Tammy, Wendy M., Wendy S. It was the best gift you could have ever given.

I thank social media where I tested samples of it, and to all my real-life friends and online friends for giving wings to my confidence.

Mostly and always, I thank God for gifting me with so much love and allowing me to experience the beauty of creativity. May these words be a credit to Him.

# Introduction

When the heart is full of gratitude, there is prayer. When the soul is full of pain, there is prayer. When it seems pointless to talk things out with other people, there is prayer. When seeking clarity on one's own feelings, there is prayer. And when there don't seem to be any words… there is prayer.

Jewish prayer gives wings to our emotions and words to our yearnings. It has the power to uplift, to articulate, to clarify. The Jewish prayer book is a window into many core concepts in our faith that warm the heart, challenge the mind, and excite the soul. Formal prayer is important, and for women, who emote instinctively and connect more readily with others, praying informally, personally, and often, can be a deeply rewarding exercise in spirituality and in our relationship with God.

Each time I pray — whether formally, from the Hebrew prayer book, or spontaneously in my own words — I feel a cleansing of the soul and a calming of the mind. God is there listening serenely, without judgment, while I step away from life's chaos for a few moments and sort through the jumble of thoughts in my brain. I thank Him for my blessings, praise Him for His greatness, and ask Him for my wish list. I pour out my pain to Him and gratefully appreciate the successes and gifts He has given me. Through this process, I come to realize how much I have to be grateful for and that He is the source of everything; that the good things in life are a gift of love, and the struggles are a learning opportunity to make me a better person. It reminds me that everything happens for a reason; that nothing is random; that the people and situations in life each have a message that I need to hear.

I walk back into real life enriched and empowered by the experience.

But the idea for this book was actually born in a conversation of frustration. Some of my friends, it seemed, did not share my love of prayer at all. They felt frustration toward prayer, for being incomprehensible. Frustration with themselves, for being unable to relate to Hebrew. Frustration with translations that still seemed like another language, as direct translations presume conceptual knowledge. There had to be a way, the conversation went, to peel back that frustration and uncover connection.

These intelligent women sought connection for their Jewish souls, regardless of education, to the ancient concepts of Jewish prayer. They sought connection for each Jewish human, to the primal emotions we all feel and need to put somewhere. They desired connection, regardless of belief system, to a higher source.

This work is my response to that need. I hold out my hand and offer you to join me in prayer. Leaf through the pages and find your point of connection — to your spiritual source, to God, to gratitude, to the calm and serenity we all seek. I join you in prayer when I say that I sincerely hope each person who turns its pages finds release from frustration and discovers those connections.

# How to Use This Book

The Hebrew prayers, as written thousands of years ago by the Men of the Great Assembly, are as potent and laden with layers of meaning as ever. They contain the richness of prophecy, the spirituality of holy people, and the universal relevance of the ages.

Yet, for many, this language is a locked garden. Whether Hebrew itself is a foreign language, or whether the concepts and references are inscrutable, some have not been able to access the beauty and meaning of this gift called the "Siddur" — the traditional Hebrew prayer book.

The composers of these original Hebrew words intended to create a vessel into which we, the users, could pour our own intent and experiences. They are a starting point, and an invitation to us to personalize them as the words move us. On any given day, I might find myself struck by a new insight into these words.

This work is intended to be a portal to that world. I invite you to read the contemporary prayers, which I offer as a window into how the prayers strike me personally. Use them as an informal meditation or, hopefully, as a bridge to eventually try out the Hebrew, with a new and fresh understanding of the theme behind the ancient words. Use them during formal services at the synagogue, to move and inspire you as you pray. Use them at home when you feel a moment of gratitude or longing. Use them right when you wake up, or perhaps just before you end your day. Or maybe when you light your Shabbat candles, you will open this book and find something that inspires you.

Know that the process and the attempt to connect with God via any means available to us is valuable and sacred. May these words find their place in your heart and help bridge you to your inner thoughts and feelings:

יִהְיוּ לְרָצוֹן אִמְרֵי פִי וְהֶגְיוֹן לִבִּי לְפָנֶיךָ, יְיָ צוּרִי וְגוֹאֲלִי.

*"May the words of my mouth and the thoughts of my heart find favor before You, God, my Rock, and my Redeemer."*

# What This Book Is Not

## THIS BOOK IS NOT A COMPLETE SIDDUR.

This book is an abridged version of the daily, Shabbat and occasional prayers. Whether it constitutes a fulfillment of one's halachic (Jewish law) obligations of prayer is subject to a variety of factors for which a qualified rabbi should be consulted. Certainly it does for mothers who are in child-rearing years. But for anyone, if it magnifies her intent and passion in prayer, allows her to pray more often or more readily, or connects her heart more strongly to her God, it will have served its purpose.

## THIS BOOK IS NOT A GRAMMATICALLY PERFECT TRANSLITERATION.

The main purpose of the transliterations in this book is to help people pronounce Hebrew. If reading Hebrew itself is unfamiliar or difficult for you, you can read the transliteration in English letters to approximate the Hebrew. Therefore, for me, perfect fidelity to grammar became less important than ease of use. The slight inconsistencies were intentional where hyphens or extra letters would facilitate ease of use, depending on context, prefixes, and suffixes.

## THIS BOOK IS NOT AN EXACT TRANSLATION.

The translation, similarly, is deliberately imperfect. There are times when I chose to extrapolate, rephrase, or summarize, where ease of use, clarity, or emotional specificity were deemed more important. I have chosen to use the Sephardic/Israeli pronunciation over the Ashkenazic version (Shabbat as opposed to Shabbos), since most English-speaking Jews are more familiar with it. There are also times and places where the translation seemed very accessible to modern thought processes and I therefore did not include a contemporary musing to match the text.

For recommended reading in terms of the complete Siddur, grammatically accurate translation, transliteration, and other forms of English-language inspiration, please see the Appendix.

## A NOTE ON TREATING THIS BOOK WITH RESPECT:

This book is not just a "book." It is a holy volume with Torah quotes that contains God's names. Therefore, it is to be treated with respect.

Other non-Torah books should not be stacked on it.

It should not be placed upside down or on the floor.

It should not be brought into a bathroom.

If it falls on the floor, it should be kissed.

If it falls into disrepair, it should not be thrown in the trash. Consult a rabbi as to its appropriate disposal.

# The Order (Siddur) of Prayer Books

The order of this prayer book, and every prayer book you will chance upon, is this: most frequently recited prayers first, followed by less frequently needed prayers, and ending with least frequently recited. Daily prayers first, weekly (Shabbat) prayers next, holiday occasions and occasional offerings last. Within those categories the prayers are arranged chronologically:

- Daily prayers: morning, afternoon, evening, night.
- Shabbat: Friday night services, Shabbat morning prayers, Shabbat afternoon prayers.
- Holidays: evening prayers first, morning prayers next, afternoon prayers last.

The word "*siddur*" itself, which is colloquial Hebrew for "prayer book," literally means "arrangement" since they are arranged in a particular order. You may notice that it's related to the word "*seder*" which also has a pre-designated order. This note should help you navigate your way more easily through various prayer books you will find yourselves reading.

*Part One:*

# DAILY PRAYERS

# Modeh Ani

*This short prayer is usually said every day, immediately upon awakening in the morning. It starts the day off with a mindset of gratitude, which is a much less stressful way to begin than checking your emails on your phone. It's a short prayer too, which means if you're just getting into prayer (or just getting back into prayer after a hiatus), it's a great thing to start with and easy to memorize.*

מוֹדָה אֲנִי לְפָנֶיךָ, מֶלֶךְ חַי וְקַיָּם, שֶׁהֶחֱזַרְתָּ בִּי נִשְׁמָתִי בְּחֶמְלָה, רַבָּה אֱמוּנָתֶךָ.

**Modeh** ani l'fanecha, melech chai v'kayam, she-hechezarta bi nishmati, b'chemla, rabbah emunatecha.

**I am grateful** before You, living and eternal King, that You have returned my soul to me with compassion. Great is Your faith in me!

Dear God,

I am so grateful for waking up this morning. Some mornings, it's so hard to get out of bed, whether because I went to bed too late, or because sometimes I feel so overwhelmed with my life that it's hard to sleep. Or maybe it's just hard for me to get out of bed and face the same old grind.

But You know what, God? I'm still grateful for the ability to wake up and have new opportunities. Thanks for believing in me. Thanks for trusting me and empowering me with another chance. Help me to make it a great day, and to remember this gratitude. Specifically, I am grateful this morning for _____.

# Asher Yatzar

This prayer is said each time one comes out of the bathroom. It is one of the most incredible prayers I know. It expresses gratitude for a healthy body — one of the most common things people take for granted.

בָּרוּךְ אַתָּה יְיָ אֱלֹהֵינוּ מֶלֶךְ הָעוֹלָם, אֲשֶׁר יָצַר אֶת הָאָדָם בְּחָכְמָה, וּבָרָא בוֹ נְקָבִים נְקָבִים, חֲלוּלִים חֲלוּלִים. גָּלוּי וְיָדוּעַ לִפְנֵי כִסֵּא כְבוֹדֶךָ, שֶׁאִם יִפָּתֵחַ אֶחָד מֵהֶם, אוֹ יִסָּתֵם אֶחָד מֵהֶם, אִי אֶפְשַׁר לְהִתְקַיֵּם וְלַעֲמוֹד לְפָנֶיךָ. בָּרוּךְ אַתָּה יְיָ, רוֹפֵא כָל בָּשָׂר וּמַפְלִיא לַעֲשׂוֹת.

**Baruch** Ata Adonoi, Elohaynu melech ha-olam, asher yatzar et ha-adam b'chochmah, u-vara vo nekavim nekavim, chalulim chalulim. Galuy v'yaduah lifnay kisay k'vo-decha, she-im yipatayach echad mayhem, o yisatem echad mayhem, ee efshar l'hitkayem v'la-amod l'fanecha. Baruch Ata Adonoi, rofay chol basar u-maflee la-asot.

**Blessed** are You, God, our God, King of the universe, Who created mankind with wisdom, and created within him many inner organs and cavities. It is obvious before Your Throne of Glory that if even one of them were to open, or if even one of them were to be blocked, it would be impossible to survive and stand here before You. Blessed are You, God, Who heals all flesh and acts wondrously.

Dear God,

I want to take a moment, right now, after I've just come out of the bathroom, to say thank You. Thank You for making my body. Thank You for making the human body so incredible, so complex, so beautiful. It is so patently clear to me that the synchronicity and order in my body is the work of Your hands. There are so many openings and so many closings, and if even one opening would wrongly close, or one closing wrongly open, everything would go so bad, so fast. So I want to thank You, God, for keeping it all moving, every second of every day, without my even thinking about it.

---

IT IS SO PATENTLY CLEAR TO ME THAT THE SYNCHRONICITY AND ORDER IN MY BODY IS THE WORK OF YOUR HANDS.

---

Thank You for healthy bodies (and in this moment I want to dedicate this prayer of gratitude to the following sick person [_____ ben/bat _____]). You create miracles daily, and I never want to forget that.

## My Soul

*One of the most core beliefs in Judaism is that each person is comprised of both body and soul. The soul is a spark of God that exists within each of us and strives for more altruism, more spirituality, and more goodness. When a person dies, the body and soul separate. The body returns to the earth and the soul ascends to the Afterlife. It's interesting that in this prayer, as in life, we use the term "me" interchangeably to refer to ourselves as our bodily selves, and as our soul-selves. We identify so strongly with both. It begs the question: am I my body or my soul? With which do I identify more? If something happened to my body, would I still be me? To my soul?*

אֱלֹהַי, נְשָׁמָה שֶׁנָּתַתָּ בִּי טְהוֹרָה הִיא. אַתָּה בְרָאתָהּ, אַתָּה יְצַרְתָּהּ, אַתָּה נְפַחְתָּהּ בִּי, וְאַתָּה מְשַׁמְּרָהּ בְּקִרְבִּי, וְאַתָּה עָתִיד

Daily Prayers    27

לִטְּלָהּ מִמֶּנִּי, וּלְהַחֲזִירָהּ בִּי לֶעָתִיד לָבוֹא. כָּל זְמַן שֶׁהַנְּשָׁמָה בְקִרְבִּי, מוֹדֶה אֲנִי לְפָנֶיךָ, יְיָ אֱלֹהַי וֵאלֹהֵי אֲבוֹתַי, רִבּוֹן כָּל הַמַּעֲשִׂים, אֲדוֹן כָּל הַנְּשָׁמוֹת. בָּרוּךְ אַתָּה יְיָ, הַמַּחֲזִיר נְשָׁמוֹת לִפְגָרִים מֵתִים.

***Elohai,*** *neshama she-natata bi tehorah hi. Ata v'rata, Ata yetzarta, Ata nefachta bi, v'Ata meshamra b'kirbi, v'Ata atid litlah mimeni, u-l'hachazira bi le-atid lavo. Kol zman she-haneshama b'kirbi, modeh ani l'fanecha, Adonoi Elohai vay-lohay avotai, Ribon kol ha-ma-asim, Adon kol ha-neshamot. Baruch Ata Adonoi, ha-machazir neshamot li-fgarim maytim.*

**My God,** the soul that You have given me is pure. You created it, You fashioned it, You blew it into me, and You safeguard it within me, and in the future, You will take it from me, and return it to me in the Afterlife. All the while that the soul is within me, I gratefully give thanks before You, my God and the God of my ancestors, God of all creations, Master of all souls. Blessed are You, God, Who restores souls to dead bodies.*

---

Dear God,

I know that Judaism talks a lot about us having a soul. Sometimes, I'm not exactly sure what that "soul" is, but I'm going to guess it's that small voice inside of me... the one that believes in me... the one that whispers words of wisdom in my ear... my true self — maybe the part of myself

---

* This reference is about the Jewish belief in the "resurrection of the dead" after the Messianic age. Our souls will be restored to us one day, and in this prayer we affirm that.

I don't share with just anyone. It's the real me, the "me" that is covered over by so many other distractions.

That soul, God, is a piece of You, and You gave it to me. Eventually You will take it from me, as I go the way of all people. But as long as that soul is within me, God, I am so grateful. It's my uniqueness, it's what makes me human and not animal, and it's the voice of conscience, of creativity, of self.

---

AS LONG AS THAT SOUL IS WITHIN ME, GOD, I AM SO GRATEFUL. IT'S MY UNIQUENESS, IT'S WHAT MAKES ME HUMAN AND NOT ANIMAL, AND IT'S THE VOICE OF CONSCIENCE, OF CREATIVITY, OF SELF.

---

Thank You, God, for giving me my soul, anew, each day.

## Torah Blessings

*The Torah is our greatest gift. It is the instruction manual for living. It addresses every aspect of the human experience. Here we remind ourselves how blessed we are to have it.*

**בָּרוּךְ** אַתָּה יְיָ אֱלֹהֵינוּ מֶלֶךְ הָעוֹלָם, אֲשֶׁר קִדְּשָׁנוּ בְּמִצְוֹתָיו, וְצִוָּנוּ לַעֲסוֹק בְּדִבְרֵי תוֹרָה.

**וְהַעֲרֶב** נָא יְיָ אֱלֹהֵינוּ אֶת דִּבְרֵי תוֹרָתְךָ בְּפִינוּ וּבְפִי עַמְּךָ בֵּית יִשְׂרָאֵל, וְנִהְיֶה אֲנַחְנוּ וְצֶאֱצָאֵינוּ וְצֶאֱצָאֵי עַמְּךָ בֵּית יִשְׂרָאֵל כֻּלָּנוּ יוֹדְעֵי שְׁמֶךָ וְלוֹמְדֵי תוֹרָתֶךָ לִשְׁמָהּ. בָּרוּךְ אַתָּה יְיָ, הַמְלַמֵּד תּוֹרָה לְעַמּוֹ יִשְׂרָאֵל.

**בָּרוּךְ** אַתָּה יְיָ אֱלֹהֵינוּ מֶלֶךְ הָעוֹלָם, אֲשֶׁר בָּחַר בָּנוּ מִכָּל הָעַמִּים, וְנָתַן לָנוּ אֶת תּוֹרָתוֹ. בָּרוּךְ אַתָּה יְיָ, נוֹתֵן הַתּוֹרָה.

**Baruch** Ata Adonoi, Elohaynu melech ha-olam, asher kid-shanu b'mitzvotav v'tzivanu la-asok b'divray Torah.

**V'ha-arev** na Adonoi Elohaynu, et divray toratcha b'finu u-b'fi amcha bait Yisrael, v'ni-hi-yeh anachnu v'tze-etza-aynu, v'tze-etza-ay amcha bait Yisrael, kulanu yoday shimecha v'lomday Torahtecha li-shma. Baruch Ata Adonoi, ha-melamed Torah la-amo Yisrael.

**Baruch** Ata Adonoi, Elohaynu Melech ha-olam, asher bachar banu mi-kol ha-amim, v'natan lanu et Torato. Baruch Ata Adonoi, notain ha-Torah.

**Blessed** are You, God, our God, King of the universe, Who has made us holy with His commandments, and commanded us to delve into the words of the Torah. Please, God, our God, make the words of Torah sweet in our mouths and in the mouths of Your people Israel, and may we, and our children, and all the children of Your people Israel, all know Your Name, and study the Torah for its own sake. Blessed are You, God, Who teaches Torah to His people Israel.

**Blessed** are You, God, our God, King of the universe, Who has chosen us from all nations, and given us the Torah. Blessed are You, God, Who gives the Torah.

Dear God,
Thank You for the gift of Torah!

I know the Torah is so important, and sometimes I feel overwhelmed with the magnitude of it all. There's so much, and humans can't always understand what's in it or what it all means, or even what Your expectations are of us. Still, I recognize that there is so much depth and beauty there, and that the true values that exist in the world today come from it. When I see the scroll in its beautiful velvet case, I am overwhelmed with love and reverence. Please allow its words to be sweet for me. Please allow my children to connect to it and recognize its value and centrality in our lives and in our faith.

---

WHEN I SEE THE SCROLL IN ITS BEAUTIFUL VELVET CASE, I AM OVERWHELMED WITH LOVE AND REVERENCE.

---

# Morning Blessings

*This series of blessings is like a journey of gratitude through our morning routine. Judaism teaches us that getting out of bed, taking steps, getting dressed, and moving on with our day, while probably rote activities (or even ones we grump about), are moments just brimming with opportunities for noticing our blessings. Some people don't have clothing. Some people can't get out of bed. Some people have back issues and can't stand up erect without pain (you may even be one of them). This segment is a neon light reminding us to slow down and notice the blessings all around us — and even inside of us.*

בָּרוּךְ אַתָּה יְיָ אֱלֹהֵינוּ מֶלֶךְ הָעוֹלָם, אֲשֶׁר נָתַן לַשֶּׂכְוִי בִינָה לְהַבְחִין בֵּין יוֹם וּבֵין לָיְלָה.

**Baruch** Ata Adonoi, Elohaynu melech ha-olam, asher natan la-sechvi vinah l'havchin bain yom u-vain layla.

**Blessed** are You, God, our God, King of the universe, Who has gifted the heart with wisdom to discern between day and night.

*Daily Prayers*

**בָּרוּךְ** אַתָּה יְיָ אֱלֹהֵינוּ מֶלֶךְ הָעוֹלָם, שֶׁלֹּא עָשַׂנִי גּוֹי.

**Baruch** Ata Adonoi, Elohaynu melech ha-olam, she-lo asani goy.

**Blessed** are You, God, our God, King of the universe, Who has not made me a non-Jew.**

**בָּרוּךְ** אַתָּה יְיָ אֱלֹהֵינוּ מֶלֶךְ הָעוֹלָם, שֶׁלֹּא עָשַׂנִי עָבֶד.

**Baruch** Ata Adonoi, Elohaynu melech ha-olam, she-lo asani aved.

**Blessed** are You, God, our God, King of the universe, Who has not made me a slave.

**בָּרוּךְ** אַתָּה יְיָ אֱלֹהֵינוּ מֶלֶךְ הָעוֹלָם, שֶׁעָשַׂנִי כִּרְצוֹנוֹ.

**Baruch** Ata Adonoi, Elohaynu melech ha-olam, she-asani kirtzono.

**Blessed** are You, God, our God, King of the universe, Who has made me exactly the way He wanted.

**בָּרוּךְ** אַתָּה יְיָ אֱלֹהֵינוּ מֶלֶךְ הָעוֹלָם, פּוֹקֵחַ עִוְרִים.

**Baruch** Ata Adonoi, Elohaynu melech ha-olam, pokayach ivrim.

**Blessed** are You, God, our God, King of the universe, Who opens the eyes of the blind.

---

** Judaism has nothing against non-Jews — in fact, it's the only one of the three major religions that teaches that non-adherents still have a place in heaven. But we are grateful that we ARE Jewish, and carry extra responsibility and privileges in being a light unto the nations.

בָּרוּךְ אַתָּה יְיָ אֱלֹהֵינוּ מֶלֶךְ הָעוֹלָם, מַלְבִּישׁ עֲרֻמִּים.

**Baruch** Ata Adonoi, Elohaynu melech ha-olam, malbish arumim.

**Blessed** are You, God, our God, King of the universe, Who clothes the naked.

בָּרוּךְ אַתָּה יְיָ אֱלֹהֵינוּ מֶלֶךְ הָעוֹלָם, מַתִּיר אֲסוּרִים.

**Baruch** Ata Adonoi, Elohaynu melech ha-olam, matir asurim.

**Blessed** are You, God, our God, King of the universe, Who releases the bound.

בָּרוּךְ אַתָּה יְיָ אֱלֹהֵינוּ מֶלֶךְ הָעוֹלָם, זוֹקֵף כְּפוּפִים.

**Baruch** Ata Adonoi, Elohaynu melech ha-olam, zokayf kefufim.

**Blessed** are You, God, our God, King of the universe, Who straightens the bent.

בָּרוּךְ אַתָּה יְיָ אֱלֹהֵינוּ מֶלֶךְ הָעוֹלָם, רוֹקַע הָאָרֶץ עַל הַמָּיִם.

**Baruch** Ata Adonoi, Elohaynu melech ha-olam, rokah ha-aretz al ha-mayim.

**Blessed** are You, God, our God, King of the universe, Who spreads out firm ground above the waters.

בָּרוּךְ אַתָּה יְיָ אֱלֹהֵינוּ מֶלֶךְ הָעוֹלָם, שֶׁעָשָׂה לִי כָּל צָרְכִּי.

**Baruch** Ata Adonoi, Elohaynu melech ha-olam, she-asa li kol tzorkee.

**Blessed** are You, God, our God, King of the universe, Who provided for all my needs.

בָּרוּךְ אַתָּה יְיָ אֱלֹהֵינוּ מֶלֶךְ הָעוֹלָם, הַמֵּכִין מִצְעֲדֵי גָבֶר.

**Baruch** Ata Adonoi, Elohaynu melech ha-olam, ha-maychin mitz-aday gaver.

**Blessed** are You, God, our God, King of the universe, Who prepares the footsteps of people.

בָּרוּךְ אַתָּה יְיָ אֱלֹהֵינוּ מֶלֶךְ הָעוֹלָם, אוֹזֵר יִשְׂרָאֵל בִּגְבוּרָה.

**Baruch** Ata Adonoi, Elohaynu melech ha-olam, ozer Yisrael b'gvurah.

**Blessed** are You, God, our God, King of the universe, Who confers strength on Israel.

בָּרוּךְ אַתָּה יְיָ אֱלֹהֵינוּ מֶלֶךְ הָעוֹלָם, עוֹטֵר יִשְׂרָאֵל בְּתִפְאָרָה.

**Baruch** Ata Adonoi, Elohaynu melech ha-olam, oter Yisrael b'tifarah.

**Blessed** are You, God, our God, King of the universe, Who crowns Israel with glory.

בָּרוּךְ אַתָּה יְיָ אֱלֹהֵינוּ מֶלֶךְ הָעוֹלָם, הַנּוֹתֵן לַיָּעֵף כֹּחַ.

**Baruch** Ata Adonoi, Elohaynu melech ha-olam, ha-notain laya-ef ko-ach.

***Blessed*** *are You, God, our God, King of the universe, Who gives energy to the weary.*

בָּרוּךְ אַתָּה יְיָ אֱלֹהֵינוּ מֶלֶךְ הָעוֹלָם, הַמַּעֲבִיר שֵׁנָה מֵעֵינַי וּתְנוּמָה מֵעַפְעַפָּי.

וִיהִי רָצוֹן מִלְּפָנֶיךָ, יְיָ אֱלֹהֵינוּ וֵאלֹהֵי אֲבוֹתֵינוּ, שֶׁתַּרְגִּילֵנוּ בְּתוֹרָתֶךָ, וְדַבְּקֵנוּ בְּמִצְוֹתֶיךָ, וְאַל תְּבִיאֵנוּ לֹא לִידֵי חֵטְא, וְלֹא לִידֵי עֲבֵרָה וְעָוֹן, וְלֹא לִידֵי נִסָּיוֹן, וְלֹא לִידֵי בִזָּיוֹן, וְאַל תַּשְׁלֶט בָּנוּ יֵצֶר הָרָע. וְהַרְחִיקֵנוּ מֵאָדָם רָע וּמֵחָבֵר רָע. וְדַבְּקֵנוּ בְּיֵצֶר הַטּוֹב וּבְמַעֲשִׂים טוֹבִים, וְכוֹף אֶת יִצְרֵנוּ לְהִשְׁתַּעְבֶּד לָךְ. וּתְנֵנוּ הַיּוֹם, וּבְכָל יוֹם, לְחֵן וּלְחֶסֶד וּלְרַחֲמִים בְּעֵינֶיךָ, וּבְעֵינֵי כָל רוֹאֵינוּ, וְתִגְמְלֵנוּ חֲסָדִים טוֹבִים. בָּרוּךְ אַתָּה יְיָ, גּוֹמֵל חֲסָדִים טוֹבִים לְעַמּוֹ יִשְׂרָאֵל.

***Baruch*** Ata Adonoi, Elohaynu melech ha-olam, ha-ma-avir shayna may-aynay u-t'numah may-afapay.

***Vihi*** ratzon mil-fanecha, Adonoi Elohaynu vay-lohay avotaynu, she-targilaynu b'Torah-techa, v'dab-kaynu b'mitzvotecha, v'al t'vi-aynu lo liday chayt, v'lo liday avayra v'avon, v'lo liday nisayon, v'lo liday vizayon, v'al tashlet banu yetzer hara. V'harchi-kaynu may-adam ra u-maychaver ra. V'dab-kaynu b'yetzer hatov u-ve-ma-asim tovim, v'chof et yitzraynu l'hishtabed lach. U-t'naynu hayom u-ve-chol yom l'chen u-l'chesed u-l'rachamim b'aynecha u-v'aynay chol ro-aynu, v'tig-milaynu chasadim tovim. Baruch Ata Adonoi, gomel chasadim tovim l'amo Yisrael.

***Blessed*** *are You, God, our God, King of the universe, Who passes sleep from before my eyes, and slumber from my eyelids.*

***And*** *may it be Your will, God, our God, and the God of our ancestors, that You make us used to Your Torah, and help us become attached to Your commandments, and don't bring us into the power of mistakes or sin, and not into the power of tests, and not into the power of humiliation, and do not let the Evil Inclination rule over us. Keep us far away from a bad person and from a bad friend. Help us stick to the Good Inclination and to good deeds, and bend our will to serve You. Give us today and every day grace, kindness, and compassion in Your eyes and in the eyes of those who see us, and bestow upon us good acts of kindness. Blessed are You, God, Who bestows good acts of kindness on His people Israel.*

Dear God,

There are so many things I do each morning that I don't even think about. I really don't want to take them for granted. As I go about my business getting ready to take on my day, there are many steps along the way, and I want to call each one out and say thank You. Here they are:

1. Thank You for giving my body and mind the wisdom to know the difference between day and night, between good and bad, between right and wrong.
2. Thank You for making me a member of the Jewish people, with mitzvot and communal responsibilities.
3. Thank You for allowing my eyes to open and function, even if I need glasses and contacts. Maybe one day I'll go for LASIK surgery, but in the meantime, help me to appreciate that there are glasses and contacts that I can wear to see normally.

4. Thank You for allowing me to have clothes to wear. I know I sometimes complain about not having enough to wear or about how much money my family members spend on clothing. But, truthfully, I recognize that these are first-world problems. Thank You for clothing that is pretty, soft, comfortable, colorful, protective, and dignified.

5. Thank You for allowing me to get out of bed and straighten my body. Thank You for a working back, for my spine, and for my bones that keep me upright.

6. Thank You for the floor and land that I can walk on. I recognize that when You first made the world, oceans covered all of it, and You then pushed back the ocean to reveal dry land that humans can walk on. I also know that when the water unnaturally comes up on the land, it's catastrophic for humans and animals. Thank You, God, for dry land and hard floors to walk on.

7. Thank You for providing for all of my needs. I have oxygen, sunshine, a brain, and food to eat. Truly, all my "needs" are met.

8. Thank You for giving strength and glory to the Jewish people. We are tiny — but tough. You have given us the ambition and drive to survive. Please let us have the strength to continue to survive and thrive.

9. Thank You for giving this tired body and brain strength, and for allowing the sleepiness of night to pass. Thanks for creating coffee! God, as I head on into this day, a lot of things are on my mind. Can I ask You for them throughout the day? I know You are there to listen to even my petty requests. Please, let my actions today be positive. Help me to not make (so many!) mistakes. Don't send me challenges that are too hard for me. Please keep me far away from bad people and bad friends. Surround me with good people, good influences, and positivity. Let the people in my life think well of me and be nice to me. Send lots of good vibes my way, God. I appreciate it!

---

SURROUND ME WITH GOOD PEOPLE, GOOD INFLUENCES, AND POSITIVITY. LET THE PEOPLE IN MY LIFE THINK WELL OF ME AND BE NICE TO ME.

---

## PRAISE OF GOD

When people think of "prayer," they usually think along the lines of, "God, gimme!" But there are actually three components of prayer: thanks for the past, praise for the present, and requests for the future. In this section, we are praising God for his kindnesses to us. Imagine if you were in a relationship (parents?) that was comprised mostly of the other person asking you for things. Not very deep or satisfying, right? Remembering to give praise where it's due is an important part of being a complete person.

## Baruch She-Amar

בָּרוּךְ שֶׁאָמַר וְהָיָה הָעוֹלָם, בָּרוּךְ הוּא, בָּרוּךְ עֹשֶׂה בְרֵאשִׁית, בָּרוּךְ אוֹמֵר וְעוֹשֶׂה, בָּרוּךְ גּוֹזֵר וּמְקַיֵּם, בָּרוּךְ מְרַחֵם עַל הָאָרֶץ, בָּרוּךְ מְרַחֵם עַל הַבְּרִיּוֹת, בָּרוּךְ מְשַׁלֵּם שָׂכָר טוֹב לִירֵאָיו, בָּרוּךְ חַי לָעַד וְקַיָּם לָנֶצַח, בָּרוּךְ פּוֹדֶה וּמַצִּיל, בָּרוּךְ שְׁמוֹ. בָּרוּךְ אַתָּה יְיָ אֱלֹהֵינוּ מֶלֶךְ הָעוֹלָם, הָאֵל הָאָב הָרַחֲמָן, הַמְהֻלָּל בְּפִי עַמּוֹ, מְשֻׁבָּח וּמְפֹאָר בִּלְשׁוֹן חֲסִידָיו וַעֲבָדָיו, וּבְשִׁירֵי דָוִד עַבְדֶּךָ. נְהַלֶּלְךָ יְיָ אֱלֹהֵינוּ בִּשְׁבָחוֹת וּבִזְמִירוֹת, וּנְגַדֶּלְךָ וּנְשַׁבֵּחֲךָ וּנְפָאֶרְךָ וְנַזְכִּיר שִׁמְךָ, וְנַמְלִיכְךָ, מַלְכֵּנוּ אֱלֹהֵינוּ, יָחִיד, חֵי הָעוֹלָמִים, מֶלֶךְ מְשֻׁבָּח וּמְפֹאָר עֲדֵי עַד שְׁמוֹ הַגָּדוֹל. בָּרוּךְ אַתָּה יְיָ, מֶלֶךְ מְהֻלָּל בַּתִּשְׁבָּחוֹת.

**Baruch** she-amar v'haya ha-olam, baruch Hu. Baruch oseh v'raysheet, baruch omer v'oseh, baruch gozer u-mekayem, baruch merachem al ha-aretz,

38   CONVERSATIONS WITH G-D

*baruch merachem al ha-briyot, baruch meshalem sachar tov li-rayav, baruch chai la-ad v'kayam la-netzach, baruch podeh u-matzil, baruch shemo. Baruch Ata Adonoi, Elohaynu melech ha-olam, ha-El ha-av ha-rachaman, ha-mehulal b'fi amo, meshubach u-mefo-ar bi-leshon chasidav va-avadav, u-v'shiray David avdecha. Ne-ha-lelcha Adonoi Elohaynu bi-shva-chot u-vi-zmirot, u-n'gad-lecha u-ni-sha-bay-chacha u-ni-fa-ercha v'nazkir shimcha, v'nam-liche-cha malkaynu Elohaynu, yachid, chay ha-olamim, melech meshubach u-mi-fo-ar aday ad sh'mo ha-gadol. Baruch Ata Adonoi, melech mehulal ba-tish-bachot.*

**Blessed** is He Who spoke and the world came to be, blessed is He. Blessed is He Who made the creation, blessed is He Who says something and does it, blessed is He who makes decrees and fulfills them, blessed is He Who has compassion on the earth, blessed is He Who has compassion on all creations, blessed is He Who pays good rewards to those who revere Him, blessed is He Who lives forever and endures for eternity, blessed is He Who redeems and saves, blessed is His name.

**Blessed** are You, God, our God, King of the universe, the God, the compassionate Father, Who is glorified by the mouth of His nation, praised and honored by the tongue of His righteous ones and servants, and with the songs of King David, Your servant. We will praise You, God, our God, with praises and songs, and declare Your greatness, and laud You, and glorify You, and mention Your name, and crown You as king, our King and God, unique, sustainer of life of all worlds, glorified and *honored King — may His name be made great forever. Blessed are You, God, the King Who is honored with praises.*

Dear God,

My job in this section of the prayers is to praise You. Frankly, that's daunting. How can I praise You when I can hardly even define You in my mind? So please, God, take this in the vein it's offered: a tiny little drop in a big, infinite bucket. A small human token to You. Thank You for understanding my smallness.

---

SO PLEASE, GOD, TAKE THIS IN THE VEIN IT'S OFFERED: A TINY LITTLE DROP IN A BIG, INFINITE BUCKET.

---

That said, God, I want to praise You for so many things. You made this world. You keep — and have always kept — Your promises to the Jewish people. You are so, so compassionate — You keep us around even though we're so flawed. You're compassionate not just to humans, but to plant life and animals, and to the entire ecosystem. You repay Your creations for their good deeds — always. You exist forever. In fact, all of our great ancestors have praised You, daily, like Abraham, Isaac, Jacob, Sarah, Rebecca, Rachel, Leah, King David, Queen Esther, and all our role models in Judaism throughout history. I want to, in my own small way, be on that train. And so, God, I will try to praise You when good things happen by saying "thank God" and meaning it. I pray, God, that there will always be people around who recognize You!

# Ashrei

*This prayer arranges praises of God in the order of the Hebrew alphabet, with one sentence of praise for each letter. Note number 16. It's the most important sentence of the prayer. Try to say it with intent and feeling.*

**אַשְׁרֵי** יוֹשְׁבֵי בֵיתֶךָ, עוֹד יְהַלְלוּךָ סֶּלָה.

אַשְׁרֵי הָעָם שֶׁכָּכָה לוֹ, אַשְׁרֵי הָעָם שֶׁיְיָ אֱלֹהָיו.

תְּהִלָּה לְדָוִד, אֲרוֹמִמְךָ אֱלוֹהַי הַמֶּלֶךְ, וַאֲבָרְכָה שִׁמְךָ לְעוֹלָם וָעֶד.

**בְּ**כָל יוֹם אֲבָרְכֶךָּ, וַאֲהַלְלָה שִׁמְךָ לְעוֹלָם וָעֶד.

**גָּ**דוֹל יְיָ וּמְהֻלָּל מְאֹד, וְלִגְדֻלָּתוֹ אֵין חֵקֶר.

**דּ**וֹר לְדוֹר יְשַׁבַּח מַעֲשֶׂיךָ, וּגְבוּרֹתֶיךָ יַגִּידוּ.

**הֲ**דַר כְּבוֹד הוֹדֶךָ, וְדִבְרֵי נִפְלְאֹתֶיךָ אָשִׂיחָה.

**וֶ**עֱזוּז נוֹרְאוֹתֶיךָ יֹאמֵרוּ, וּגְדֻלָּתְךָ אֲסַפְּרֶנָּה.

**זֵ**כֶר רַב טוּבְךָ יַבִּיעוּ, וְצִדְקָתְךָ יְרַנֵּנוּ.

**חַ**נּוּן וְרַחוּם יְיָ, אֶרֶךְ אַפַּיִם וּגְדָל חָסֶד.

**ט**וֹב יְיָ לַכֹּל, וְרַחֲמָיו עַל כָּל מַעֲשָׂיו.

**י**וֹדוּךָ יְיָ כָּל מַעֲשֶׂיךָ, וַחֲסִידֶיךָ יְבָרְכוּכָה.

**כְּ**בוֹד מַלְכוּתְךָ יֹאמֵרוּ, וּגְבוּרָתְךָ יְדַבֵּרוּ.

**לְ**הוֹדִיעַ לִבְנֵי הָאָדָם גְּבוּרֹתָיו, וּכְבוֹד הֲדַר מַלְכוּתוֹ.

**מַ**לְכוּתְךָ מַלְכוּת כָּל עוֹלָמִים, וּמֶמְשַׁלְתְּךָ בְּכָל דֹּר וָדֹר.

**ס**וֹמֵךְ יְיָ לְכָל הַנֹּפְלִים, וְזוֹקֵף לְכָל הַכְּפוּפִים.

**עֵ**ינֵי כֹל אֵלֶיךָ יְשַׂבֵּרוּ, וְאַתָּה נוֹתֵן לָהֶם אֶת אָכְלָם בְּעִתּוֹ.

**פּ**וֹתֵחַ אֶת יָדֶךָ, וּמַשְׂבִּיעַ לְכָל חַי רָצוֹן.

**צַ**דִּיק יְיָ בְּכָל דְּרָכָיו, וְחָסִיד בְּכָל מַעֲשָׂיו.

**קָ**רוֹב יְיָ לְכָל קֹרְאָיו, לְכֹל אֲשֶׁר יִקְרָאֻהוּ בֶאֱמֶת.

**רְ**צוֹן יְרֵאָיו יַעֲשֶׂה, וְאֶת שַׁוְעָתָם יִשְׁמַע וְיוֹשִׁיעֵם.

שׁוֹמֵר יְיָ אֶת כָּל אֹהֲבָיו, וְאֵת כָּל הָרְשָׁעִים יַשְׁמִיד.

תְּהִלַּת יְיָ יְדַבֶּר פִּי, וִיבָרֵךְ כָּל בָּשָׂר שֵׁם קָדְשׁוֹ לְעוֹלָם וָעֶד.

וַאֲנַחְנוּ נְבָרֵךְ יָהּ, מֵעַתָּה וְעַד עוֹלָם, הַלְלוּיָהּ.

**Ashrei** yoshvay vay-techa, od yehalelucha selah.
Ashrei ha-am she-kacha lo, ashrei ha-am she-Adonoi Elohav.
Tehilla l'David, aromimcha Elohai ha-melech, va-avarcha shimcha l'olam va-ed.
B'chol yom avar-checka, va-ahalelah shimcha l'olam va-ed.
Gadol Adonoi u-mehulal me-od, v'li-g'dulato ayn cheker.
Dor l'dor yishabach ma-asecha, u-g'vurotecha yagidu.
Hadar ke-vod hodecha, v'divray nif-le-otecha asicha.
Ve-ezuz noratecha yomayru, u-g'dulatcha asaprena.
Zecher rav tuvcha yabi-u, v'tzid-katcha y'ranenu.
Chanun v'rachum Adonoi, erech apayim u-g'dal chased.
Tov Adonoi la-kol, v'rachamav al kol ma'asav.
Yoducha Adonoi kol ma-asecha, va-cha-sidecha y'var-chucha.
Ke-vod malchutcha yomayru, u-g'vuratcha y'daberu.
L'hodi-ya livnay ha-adam g'vurotav, u-k'vod hadar malchuto.
Malchut-cha malchut kol olamim, u-mem-shal-t'cha b'chol dor va-dor.
Somech Adonoi l'chol ha-noflim, v'zokef l'kol ha-k'fufim.
Aynay chol ay-lecha y'saberu, v'Ata notayn lahem et ochlam b'ito.
Potayach et yadecha, u-masbia l'chol chai ratzon.
Tzadik Adonoi b'chol d'rachav, v'chasid b'chol ma'asav.
Karov Adonoi l'chol kor'av, l'chol asher yikra-uhu v'emet.
Ritzon yerayav ya'aseh, v'et shav'atam yishma v'yoshi'aym.

*Shomer Adonoi et kol ohavav, v'ayt kol ha-resha'im yashmid. Tehilat Adonoi y'daber pi, vi-varaych kol basar shem kadsho l'olam va'ed.*

*Va'anachnu n'varech Yah, me'ata v'ad olam, halleluyah.*

1. Your nation, God, is lucky to be Jewish.
2. I will praise You daily.
3. You are so great, God, that truly I couldn't even fathom You if I tried.
4. You are not just praised in one generation, but You are praised in each generation.
5. People have always praised Your glory and miracles.
6. They have praised You, and I, too, will tell stories of the small miracles that happen to me in my life.
7. People have always remembered the past kindnesses You have done, and those memories make them so happy.
8. God, You are kind and compassionate. You are patient with us when we fail our challenges.
9. God, You are good to all — humans, animals, and plant life.
10. All of Your creations praise You. Animals sing praise to You in their own language. Even the sounds of the waves crashing and the breeze blowing are a form of praise to You.
11. The people, animals, and the earth itself are singing songs of Your majesty and greatness. Who else could create such an incredible world?
12. They want to let the whole world know of Your greatness and honor.
13. This majesty, God, is an eternal one — not like human kingdoms that rise and fall.

*Daily Prayers*

14. God, You lift up those that have fallen.

15. Everyone looks hopefully toward You, and You don't disappoint — You feed the world, each creature according to its needs.

16. You open Your hand and sustain us all with exactly what we need in our lives.

17. God, You never make mistakes. All Your deeds are pure goodness, even if they don't seem so to us.

18. You are close to anyone who calls to You and wants a relationship. All they need to do is talk to You sincerely, and You're there.

19. You do the will of those who revere You, and You hear their voice whenever they speak to You — and You respond in Your decisions and actions!

20. God protects those who love Him, and destroys evil.

21. I wish for myself that I always remember to praise and thank God for all the good that is in my life, and to never take it for granted.

22. I wish, too, that everyone could know and appreciate Your existence, God, but meanwhile I will try to do my share and lead by example.

## Halleluyah

This famous word literally means "praise God." There are five chapters of Psalms that start and end with this word — in fact, they're the last five chapters out of one hundred and fifty in total of the entire book of Psalms. This is the last one — Psalm 150. It's a joyous expression of showing God praise with music and singing.

**הַלְלוּיָהּ,** הַלְלוּ אֵל בְּקָדְשׁוֹ, הַלְלוּהוּ בִּרְקִיעַ עֻזּוֹ. הַלְלוּהוּ בִגְבוּרֹתָיו, הַלְלוּהוּ כְּרֹב גֻּדְלוֹ. הַלְלוּהוּ בְּתֵקַע שׁוֹפָר, הַלְלוּהוּ בְּנֵבֶל וְכִנּוֹר. הַלְלוּהוּ בְּתֹף וּמָחוֹל, הַלְלוּהוּ בְּמִנִּים וְעֻגָב. הַלְלוּהוּ בְצִלְצְלֵי שָׁמַע, הַלְלוּהוּ בְּצִלְצְלֵי תְרוּעָה. כֹּל הַנְּשָׁמָה תְּהַלֵּל יָהּ הַלְלוּיָהּ. כֹּל הַנְּשָׁמָה תְּהַלֵּל יָהּ הַלְלוּיָהּ.

**Halleluyah,** *halelu El b'kadsho, halleluhu bi-reki-ya uzo. Halleluhu b'g'vurotav, halleluhu k'rov gudlo. Halleluhu b'tayka shofar, halleluhu b'nayvel v'chinor, halleluhu b'tof u-machol, halleluhu b'minim v'ugav. Halleluhu b'tzil-tz'lay shama, halleluhu b'tzil-tz'lay terua. Kol ha-neshama t'hallel Yah, halleluyah. Kol ha-neshama t'hallel Yah, halleluyah.*

**Praise** *God! Praise God in His holy place, praise God in His heavens of power. Praise God for His strength, praise God as befits His greatness. Praise Him with the sound of the shofar, praise Him with the lyre and harp. Praise Him with drum and dance, praise Him with organ and flute. Praise Him with cymbal crashes; praise Him with trumpet sounds. May all souls praise God, praise God! May all souls praise God, praise God!*

God, after concentrating on all the things I have to be grateful for, I feel like I should literally sing and dance to say thank You! When the Temple in Jerusalem was standing, the Levites would play many beautiful instruments. Music is such a powerful force, and specifically, a spiritual force. If I could, I would thank You, God, with beautiful music — with shofar sounds, harp, lyre, drums, organs, flutes, and dancing. I would play for You cymbals and trumpets.

*Daily Prayers*

---

## MUSIC IS SUCH A POWERFUL FORCE, AND SPECIFICALLY A SPIRITUAL FORCE.

---

I wish everyone in the world could appreciate You, God.

# *Yishtabach*

*This well-known prayer concludes the section of praise.*

יִשְׁתַּבַּח שִׁמְךָ לָעַד מַלְכֵּנוּ, הָאֵל הַמֶּלֶךְ הַגָּדוֹל וְהַקָּדוֹשׁ בַּשָּׁמַיִם וּבָאָרֶץ. כִּי לְךָ נָאֶה, יְיָ אֱלֹהֵינוּ וֵאלֹהֵי אֲבוֹתֵינוּ, שִׁיר וּשְׁבָחָה, הַלֵּל וְזִמְרָה, עֹז וּמֶמְשָׁלָה, נֶצַח, גְּדֻלָּה וּגְבוּרָה, תְּהִלָּה וְתִפְאֶרֶת, קְדֻשָּׁה וּמַלְכוּת. בְּרָכוֹת וְהוֹדָאוֹת מֵעַתָּה וְעַד עוֹלָם. בָּרוּךְ אַתָּה יְיָ, אֵל מֶלֶךְ גָּדוֹל בַּתִּשְׁבָּחוֹת, אֵל הַהוֹדָאוֹת, אֲדוֹן הַנִּפְלָאוֹת, הַבּוֹחֵר בְּשִׁירֵי זִמְרָה, מֶלֶךְ, אֵל, חֵי הָעוֹלָמִים.

**Yishtabach** shimcha la-ad malkaynu. Ha-el, ha-melech, ha-gadol v'ha-kadosh, ba-shamayim u-va-aretz. Ki l'cha na-eh Adonoi Elohaynu vay-lohay avotaynu, shir u-shvacha, halel v'zimra, oz u-memshala, netzach, gedula, u-g'vura, tehila v'tiferet, kedusha u-malchut. Brachot v'hoda-ot may-ata v'ad olam. Baruch Ata Adonoi, El melech gadol ba-tishbachot, El ha-hoda-ot, Adon ha-nifla-ot, ha-bocher b'shiray zimra, melech, El, chay ha-olamim.

**May** Your name be praised forever, our King, God, great and holy King, in the heavens and earth. Because *it's befitting for You, God, our God, and the God of our ancestors, song and praise, glorification and hymns, strength and dominion, eternity, greatness, power, praise and splendor, holiness and royalty, blessings and gratitude from now until forever. Blessed are You God, God, King Who is made great with praises, God of thanksgivings, master of wonders, Who chooses songs of musical praises, King, God, provider of life for all the world.*

God, I am picturing in my mind You, sitting on a throne, listening to all of us here down below. It's scary, and at the same time awesomely inspiring. You live forever, while we are so small and finite. Really, all the creatures of the world should praise, thank, glorify, adore, bless, and sing to You — way beyond the vocabulary that is available to me, and even beyond the beautiful Hebrew words of Psalms written by King David himself.

> GOD, I AM PICTURING IN MY MIND YOU, SITTING ON A THRONE, LISTENING TO ALL OF US HERE DOWN BELOW. IT'S SCARY, AND AT THE SAME TIME AWESOMELY INSPIRING.

Even though I am totally incapable of doing all of that, nor would I know how, the fact remains that You deserve to be praised — today and forever. In every moment I should be offering You song and praise, hymns, and descriptions of Your power, dominion, triumph, greatness, strength, splendor, holiness, sovereignty, blessings and thanksgivings — from now till forever. So what I'll do is this, then: I will simply say, I thank and bless You, God — because ultimately it is only You Who gives life to the entire world.

# Shema

*The prayer book includes a selection of prayers both before and after the Shema. The Shema is really about awareness of God — that He is one God, and not more, and that He alone is the singular and unique unifying force of everything. There are three ways of recognizing God: through nature, through Torah, and by seeing His hand throughout history. The pre-Shema prayers focus on the first two.*

## NATURE:

You, God, created this incredible physical world of sun, moon, and stars; of heaven and earth. Every day You choose to renew the workings of the world. This world of science is so full of wisdom and complexity, it astounds me anew each time I think of it. The celestial beings, we are taught, "praise" You in their own soundless way as they wax and wane, shine and fade, and bear testament to Your creativity.

In the spiritual world, God, the angels also praise You! They line up in their perfect way and proclaim Your praises. They accept upon themselves Your kingship — as should we — and with tranquility, sweetness, and articulation, literally sing the following song:

"Holy, holy, holy is God — the whole world is filled with His glory."

Then other groups of angels raise themselves up and continue the song, saying:

"Blessed is the glory of God from His place."

In this conversation, God, the angels are expressing that it's You alone Who effects deeds, Who creates new things, Who is too awesome even for praise.

God, I bless You for creating this incredible world of nature; of the sun, moon, and stars that we can see; of the angels that we cannot see; of everything in between — and for keeping it all turning, every single day. Nature is a gift by which I can understand You.

TORAH:

**אַהֲבָה** רַבָּה אֲהַבְתָּנוּ, יְיָ אֱלֹהֵינוּ, חֶמְלָה גְדוֹלָה וִיתֵרָה חָמַלְתָּ עָלֵינוּ. אָבִינוּ מַלְכֵּנוּ, בַּעֲבוּר אֲבוֹתֵינוּ שֶׁבָּטְחוּ בְךָ, וַתְּלַמְּדֵם חֻקֵּי חַיִּים, כֵּן תְּחָנֵּנוּ וּתְלַמְּדֵנוּ. אָבִינוּ, הָאָב הָרַחֲמָן, הַמְרַחֵם, רַחֵם עָלֵינוּ, וְתֵן בְּלִבֵּנוּ לְהָבִין וּלְהַשְׂכִּיל, לִשְׁמֹעַ, לִלְמֹד וּלְלַמֵּד, לִשְׁמֹר וְלַעֲשׂוֹת וּלְקַיֵּם אֶת כָּל דִּבְרֵי תַלְמוּד תּוֹרָתֶךָ בְּאַהֲבָה. וְהָאֵר עֵינֵינוּ בְּתוֹרָתֶךָ, וְדַבֵּק לִבֵּנוּ בְּמִצְוֹתֶיךָ, וְיַחֵד לְבָבֵנוּ לְאַהֲבָה וּלְיִרְאָה אֶת שְׁמֶךָ, וְלֹא נֵבוֹשׁ לְעוֹלָם וָעֶד. כִּי בְשֵׁם קָדְשְׁךָ הַגָּדוֹל וְהַנּוֹרָא בָּטָחְנוּ, נָגִילָה וְנִשְׂמְחָה בִּישׁוּעָתֶךָ. וַהֲבִיאֵנוּ לְשָׁלוֹם מֵאַרְבַּע כַּנְפוֹת הָאָרֶץ, וְתוֹלִיכֵנוּ קוֹמְמִיּוּת לְאַרְצֵנוּ, כִּי אֵל פּוֹעֵל יְשׁוּעוֹת אָתָּה, וּבָנוּ בָחַרְתָּ מִכָּל עַם וְלָשׁוֹן. וְקֵרַבְתָּנוּ לְשִׁמְךָ הַגָּדוֹל סֶלָה בֶּאֱמֶת, לְהוֹדוֹת לְךָ וּלְיַחֶדְךָ בְּאַהֲבָה. בָּרוּךְ אַתָּה יְיָ, הַבּוֹחֵר בְּעַמּוֹ יִשְׂרָאֵל בְּאַהֲבָה.

***Ahava*** raba ahavtanu, Adonoi Elohaynu. Chemla gedola vi-tayra chamalta alaynu. Avinu malkaynu, ba-avur avotaynu she-batchu v'cha va-telamdaym chukay chaim, ken t'chanaynu u-t'lam-daynu. Avinu, ha-av ha-rachaman, ha-merachem rachem alaynu, v'tayn b'libaynu vina, l'havin u-l'haskil. Li-shmo-a, lil-mod u-l'lamed, li-shmor v'la-asot, u-l'ka-yem et kol divray talmud Torah-techa b'ahava. V'ha-er aynaynu b'Torah-techa, v'dabek libaynu b'mitzvotecha, v'yached le-vavaynu l'ahava u-l'yira et sh'mecha, v'lo nayvosh l'olam va-ed. Ki v'shem kadshecha ha-gadol, v'hanora batachnu, nageela v'nis-micha bi-shu-atecha. V'havi-aynu l'shalom may-arba

*Daily Prayers*

kanfot ha-aretz, v'tolichaynu komemiyut l'artzaynu, ki El po-el yeshuot Ata, u-vanu vacharta mikol am v'lashon. V'kayravtanu l'shimcha hagadol selah va-emet, l'hodot l'cha u-l'yachedcha b'ahava. Baruch Ata Adonoi, ha-bocher b'amo Yisrael b'ahava.

**With** a great love You have loved us, God, our God. You've bestowed on us great and overly abundant compassion. Our Father, our King, for the sake of our ancestors who trusted in You, and You taught them the laws of life, so too, give us favor and teach us too. Our Father, Father of compassion, Who has mercy — have mercy on us, and instill in our hearts insight to understand and be wise. To listen, to learn, and to teach, to keep and to do and to fulfill, all the words of the lessons of Your Torah with love. Enlighten our eyes in Your Torah; connect our hearts to Your mitzvot; bring our hearts to be one with love and revere Your name, and may we never feel shame forever. For we have trusted in Your holy, great, and awesome name, and we'll rejoice and be happy in Your salvation. Bring us in peace from the four corners of the earth, and lead us proudly to our Land, for You are a worker of redemption, and You have chosen us from all nations and peoples. And bring us close to Your great name forever and in truth, to praise You and unify You in love. Blessed are You, God, Who chooses His nation Israel in love.

You love us so much, God — and this is why You have given us a Torah. The Torah is the intellectual way that we can perceive Your wisdom. God, have compassion on us, and teach us. Instill in our hearts and in the hearts of our children and loved ones, to understand and to elucidate, to listen, learn, teach, safeguard, perform, and fulfill all the words of the Torah, with love. Enlighten us in Your Torah — it can be so vast and hard to access. Make it accessible, interesting, and relevant to us. Provide teachers who can explain it to us. Allow us to do the mitzvot that You've given us with joy, knowledge, and pride. Instill in our hearts the desire to love You, Your Torah, and our faith — from a place of intellect and education. We don't ever want to feel embarrassed at our ignorance. Thank You, God, for choosing the Jewish people with love.

---

ALLOW US TO DO THE MITZVOT THAT YOU'VE GIVEN US WITH JOY, KNOWLEDGE, AND PRIDE.

---

The Shema itself consists of the six-word mantra of Jews worldwide — our declaration of God's oneness and uniqueness. The line that appears after it is said in a whisper. Afterwards follow three paragraphs. The first is about loving God; the second is about rewards and consequences; and the third is about remembering God and his commandments. These famous words are written in scrolls inside of *mezuzah* cases and *tefillin* (phylacteries) that are wrapped with black straps around the head and arm while praying.

שְׁמַע | יִשְׂרָאֵל, יְיָ | אֱלֹהֵינוּ, יְיָ | אֶחָד.

בָּרוּךְ שֵׁם כְּבוֹד מַלְכוּתוֹ לְעוֹלָם וָעֶד.

**Shema** *Yisrael, Adonoi Elohaynu, Adonoi echad.*

*Baruch shem k'vod malchuto l'olam va-ed.*

**Hear,** *O Israel, God is our God; God is One.*

*Blessed is the name of the honor of His kingdom for all eternity.*

LOVE:

וְאָהַבְתָּ אֵת יְיָ ׀ אֱלֹהֶיךָ, בְּכָל ׀ לְבָבְךָ, וּבְכָל נַפְשְׁךָ, וּבְכָל מְאֹדֶךָ. וְהָיוּ הַדְּבָרִים הָאֵלֶּה, אֲשֶׁר ׀ אָנֹכִי מְצַוְּךָ הַיּוֹם, עַל ׀ לְבָבֶךָ. וְשִׁנַּנְתָּם לְבָנֶיךָ, וְדִבַּרְתָּ בָּם, בְּשִׁבְתְּךָ בְּבֵיתֶךָ, וּבְלֶכְתְּךָ בַדֶּרֶךְ, וּבְשָׁכְבְּךָ, וּבְקוּמֶךָ. וּקְשַׁרְתָּם לְאוֹת ׀ עַל יָדֶךָ, וְהָיוּ לְטֹטָפֹת בֵּין ׀ עֵינֶיךָ. וּכְתַבְתָּם ׀ עַל מְזֻזוֹת בֵּיתֶךָ וּבִשְׁעָרֶיךָ.

**V'ahavta** ayt Adonoi Elohecha, b'chol l'vav-cha, u-v'chol naf-sh'cha, u-v'chol m'odecha. V'hayu ha-d'varim ha-ayleh, asher anochi m'tzav-cha ha-yom, al l'vavecha. V'shi-nantam l'vanecha v'dibarta bam, b'shiv-t'cha b'vay-techa u-v'lech-t'cha va-derech, u-v'shach-b'cha u-v'kumecha. U-k'shartam l'ot al yadecha, v'hayu l'totafot bayn aynecha. U-ch'tavtam al mezuzot baytecha u-visharecha.

**You shall** love God, your God with all your heart and with all your soul and with all your might. May these words that I am commanding you today be on your heart. Teach them to your children and speak of them when you sit in your home and when you travel on the road; when you lie down and when you arise. Tie them as a sign on your arm and may they be phylacteries between your eyes. And write them on mezuzah scrolls on the doorposts of your homes and gates.

God, the concept of loving You can be hard — how does one love a "Being" that cannot be grasped with the five senses? But I am going to try, God — with all my heart, soul, and energy. I would like to become more connected to this idea, not just at synagogue, but at home. Not just for me, but to speak of it openly with my children. Not just on special occasions, but daily. And God, when I see the mezuzah on my door, whose scroll contains these concepts, I will remember that my home is an oasis of spirituality and God-awareness in a sad and sometimes empty and confusing world.

Thank You, God, for the gift of loving You.

## REWARDS AND CONSEQUENCES:

וְהָיָה אִם שָׁמֹעַ תִּשְׁמְעוּ אֶל מִצְוֹתַי, אֲשֶׁר | אָנֹכִי מְצַוֶּה | אֶתְכֶם הַיּוֹם, לְאַהֲבָה אֶת יְיָ | אֱלֹהֵיכֶם וּלְעָבְדוֹ, בְּכָל | לְבַבְכֶם וּבְכָל נַפְשְׁכֶם. וְנָתַתִּי מְטַר | אַרְצְכֶם בְּעִתּוֹ, יוֹרֶה וּמַלְקוֹשׁ, וְאָסַפְתָּ דְגָנֶךָ וְתִירֹשְׁךָ וְיִצְהָרֶךָ. וְנָתַתִּי | עֵשֶׂב | בְּשָׂדְךָ לִבְהֶמְתֶּךָ, וְאָכַלְתָּ וְשָׂבָעְתָּ. הִשָּׁמְרוּ לָכֶם פֶּן יִפְתֶּה לְבַבְכֶם, וְסַרְתֶּם וַעֲבַדְתֶּם | אֱלֹהִים | אֲחֵרִים וְהִשְׁתַּחֲוִיתֶם לָהֶם. וְחָרָה | אַף יְיָ בָּכֶם, וְעָצַר | אֶת הַשָּׁמַיִם וְלֹא יִהְיֶה מָטָר, וְהָאֲדָמָה לֹא תִתֵּן אֶת יְבוּלָהּ, וַאֲבַדְתֶּם | מְהֵרָה מֵעַל הָאָרֶץ הַטֹּבָה | אֲשֶׁר | יְיָ נֹתֵן לָכֶם. וְשַׂמְתֶּם | אֶת דְּבָרַי | אֵלֶּה עַל | לְבַבְכֶם וְעַל נַפְשְׁכֶם, וּקְשַׁרְתֶּם | אֹתָם לְאוֹת | עַל יֶדְכֶם, וְהָיוּ לְטוֹטָפֹת בֵּין | עֵינֵיכֶם. וְלִמַּדְתֶּם | אֹתָם | אֶת בְּנֵיכֶם לְדַבֵּר בָּם, בְּשִׁבְתְּךָ בְּבֵיתֶךָ, וּבְלֶכְתְּךָ בַדֶּרֶךְ, וּבְשָׁכְבְּךָ, וּבְקוּמֶךָ. וּכְתַבְתָּם | עַל מְזוּזוֹת בֵּיתֶךָ וּבִשְׁעָרֶיךָ. לְמַעַן | יִרְבּוּ | יְמֵיכֶם וִימֵי בְנֵיכֶם | עַל הָאֲדָמָה | אֲשֶׁר | נִשְׁבַּע | יְיָ לַאֲבֹתֵיכֶם לָתֵת לָהֶם, כִּימֵי הַשָּׁמַיִם | עַל הָאָרֶץ.

**V'haya** im shamo-a tish-m'u el mitz-vo-tai, asher anochi m'tzaveh etchem hayom, l'ahava et Adonoi Elohaychem u-l'avdo b'chol l'vav-chem u-v'chol naf-sh'chem. V'natati m'tar artzechem b'ito, yoreh u-malkosh, v'asafta d'ganecha v'tirosh-cha v'yitz-harecha. V'natati ay-sev b'sadcha liv-hem-techa,

Daily Prayers 53

*v'achalta v'savata. Hi-shamru lachem pen yifteh l'vav-chem, v'sartem va-ava-d'tem elohim acherim v'hish-ta-cha-vitem lahem. V'chara af Adonoi bachem, v'atzar et ha-shamayim v'lo y'hi-yeh matar, v'ha-adama lo titen et yevula, va-ava-d'tem m'hayra may-al ha-aretz ha-tova asher Adonoi notayn lachem. V'samtem et d'varai ayleh al l'vav-chem v'al naf-shechem, u-k'shartem otam l'ot al yedchem, v'hayu l'totafot bayn ay-naychem. V'lima-d'tem otam et b'naychem l'daber bam, b'shivt'cha b'vaytecha, u-v'lecht'cha ba-derech, u-v'shachb'cha u-v'kumecha. U-ch'tav-tam al mezuzot baytecha u-visharecha. L'maan yirbu y'maychem vimay v'naychem al ha-adama asher nishba Adonoi la-avotaychem la-tayt lahem kimay ha-shamayim al ha-aretz.*

**And it shall be**, if you listen well to my commandments that I'm commanding you today, to love God, your God and to serve Him with all your heart and all your soul — then I will give rain to your land in its time, the early and late rains, and you will gather your grain, wine and oil. I will give grass in your fields for your animals, and you will eat and be satisfied. Watch yourself, or your hearts will swerve, and you'll turn and worship false gods and bow down to them. God will become very angry with you, and He will close up the heavens and there will be no rain, and the earth will not give its bounty. You will be quickly banished from the good land that God gave you. Put these words on your heart and on your soul; tie them as a sign on your arms; let them be phylacteries between your eyes. Teach them to your children to speak of them, when you are sitting in your homes or *traveling on the road; when you lie down and when you get up. Write them on the doorposts of your homes and gates — in order that your days and the days of your children be many on the land that God promised your ancestors to give them, like the days of the heavens on the earth.*

God, you have promised in Your Torah that our actions matter. Our good deeds, when we soar above our nature, and listen to our small, still, soul-voice, will be rewarded. And, our mistakes and misdeeds will incur consequences. I know I need to be careful. I need to learn to avoid people and situations that don't bring out the best in me. I have to remind these words to travel from my head to my heart so I can become the best me. I need to teach them to my children, and discuss them regularly, again, not just at synagogue, but at home. When I get up and go to bed. These are the most important concepts of life.

REMEMBERING:

**וַיֹּאמֶר** | יְיָ | אֶל מֹשֶׁה לֵּאמֹר. דַּבֵּר | אֶל בְּנֵי | יִשְׂרָאֵל וְאָמַרְתָּ אֲלֵהֶם, וְעָשׂוּ לָהֶם צִיצִת עַל כַּנְפֵי | בִגְדֵיהֶם לְדֹרֹתָם, וְנָתְנוּ | עַל צִיצִת הַכָּנָף פְּתִיל תְּכֵלֶת. וְהָיָה לָכֶם לְצִיצִת, וּרְאִיתֶם | אֹתוֹ וּזְכַרְתֶּם | אֶת כָּל מִצְוֹת | יְיָ, וַעֲשִׂיתֶם | אֹתָם, וְלֹא תָתוּרוּ | אַחֲרֵי לְבַבְכֶם וְאַחֲרֵי | עֵינֵיכֶם, אֲשֶׁר אַתֶּם זֹנִים | אַחֲרֵיהֶם. לְמַעַן תִּזְכְּרוּ וַעֲשִׂיתֶם | אֶת כָּל מִצְוֹתָי, וִהְיִיתֶם קְדֹשִׁים לֵאלֹהֵיכֶם. אֲנִי יְיָ | אֱלֹהֵיכֶם, אֲשֶׁר הוֹצֵאתִי | אֶתְכֶם | מֵאֶרֶץ מִצְרַיִם, לִהְיוֹת לָכֶם לֵאלֹהִים, אֲנִי | יְיָ | אֱלֹהֵיכֶם.

**Va-yomer** Adonoi el Moshe lay-mor. Daber el bnai Yisrael v'amarta alayhem v'asu lahem tzitzit al kanfay vig-dayhem l'dorotam. V'natnu al ha-tzitzit ha-kanaf p'til t'chaylet. V'haya lachem l'tzitzit, u-r'item

Daily Prayers

oto u-z'chartem et kol mitzvot Adonoi, va-asitem otam, v'lo taturu acharay l'vav-chem v'acharay ay-nay-chem, asher atem zonim acharay-hem. L'ma-an tizk'ru va-asitem et kol mitzvotai, v'hi-yitem kedoshim lay-lohaychem. Ani Adonoi Elohaychem asher hotzayti etchem may-eretz mitzrayim li-hi-yot lahem lay-lohim. Ani Adonoi Elohaychem.

**And** God said to Moses as follows: speak to the people of Israel, and tell them to make themselves tzitzit — fringes — on the corners of their clothing forever. They should tie onto the fringes of each corner a blue string called "t'chaylet." It will be fringes for you, and you'll see them and remember all the commandments of God, and do them, and you will not turn after your heart and after your eyes, which you're straying after. In order that you may remember and do all of my commandments, and be holy to your God. I am God, your God, Who has taken you out of the land of Egypt to be your God. I am God, your God.

God, in this final paragraph of the Shema, the least-known one, You ask us to remember all that You've instructed us. And You've given us a pretty specific method to remember: to wear *tzitzit*. This is a mitzvah that when we wear a four-cornered garment, we should tie fringes in a special way on each corner. That some fringes should be blue. Then when we look at that color blue, we will remember the heavens and ultimately, You. But whether I have four-cornered garments or not, I recognize, God, how important it is to remember. To remember that which is important and not let it get swept away in all the silly urgencies of our lives. To make sure that no matter who we are, how we think, or what makes us tick, we will do what it takes to remember these ideas: that You, God made us. That

You love us. That You expect us to take the high road. Not to follow our hearts and whims but instead to listen to our minds and souls… and to be proud, today and always, to be called Your people.

POST-SHEMA THOUGHTS:

God, here I am, just coming off the Shema and preparing for the pinnacle of the prayer: the Amidah.

So before we all rise as a congregation to do so, or before I rise on my own, I'd like to state my affirmation of the truth of the Shema I just said, and of the more private words I am about to say personally in the Amidah. I affirm that all of it is true, although I struggle to understand it sometimes. All of it is true, although I fail to truly believe it sometimes. All of it is true, though so much about contemporary life conspires against it sometimes.

It's true, God, that You're it. You're the One Who makes it all happen. And just as You took us out of Egypt all those years ago, Your justice today reigns from one end of the earth to the other. Back in Egypt, God, the Jews sang to You. They sang about Your great deeds and about Your righteousness. They sang about how You lift those who feel low; how You liberate humanity from captivity both actual and figurative; how You help the needy; how You listen to the cries of those who are broken. They sang that song then, God, and we sing it again right here.

# Mi Kamocha

מִי כָמֹכָה בָּאֵלִם יְיָ, מִי כָּמֹכָה נֶאְדָּר בַּקֹּדֶשׁ, נוֹרָא תְהִלֹּת, עֹשֵׂה פֶלֶא.

שִׁירָה חֲדָשָׁה שִׁבְּחוּ גְאוּלִים לְשִׁמְךָ עַל שְׂפַת הַיָּם, יַחַד כֻּלָּם הוֹדוּ וְהִמְלִיכוּ וְאָמְרוּ: יְיָ יִמְלֹךְ לְעֹלָם וָעֶד.

*Daily Prayers*

***Mi*** *kamocha ba-aylim Adonoi? Mi kamocha ne-edar ba-kodesh? Nora tehilot oseh feleh. Shira chadasha shibchu ge-ulim l'shimcha al sfat ha-yam, yachad kulam hodu v'himlichu, v'amru. Adonoi yimloch l'olam va-ed!*

**Who** is like You among the powers, God? Who is like You, mighty in holiness? You are too awesome for praise, and You act wondrously. The redeemed ones [in Egypt] praised You with a new song at the shore of the sea. Together, they all praised and coronated You.

Who is like You, God? Who can possibly achieve what You do? On that day, back in Egypt, that was a new song to You that no one had ever sung, and today we sing it too, as an ancient reminder of that truth. I affirm, God, that just as that song has endured from then until now, may it endure forever. May there always be people around to sing that very song!

---

I AFFIRM, GOD, THAT JUST AS THAT SONG HAS ENDURED FROM THEN UNTIL NOW, MAY IT ENDURE FOREVER.

---

## Tzur Yisrael

צוּר יִשְׂרָאֵל, קוּמָה בְּעֶזְרַת יִשְׂרָאֵל, וּפְדֵה כִנְאֻמֶךָ יְהוּדָה וְיִשְׂרָאֵל. גֹּאֲלֵנוּ יְיָ צְבָאוֹת שְׁמוֹ, קְדוֹשׁ יִשְׂרָאֵל. בָּרוּךְ אַתָּה יְיָ גָּאַל יִשְׂרָאֵל.

***Tzur*** *Yisrael, kuma b'ezrat Yisrael, u-fday chinumecha Yehuda v'Yisrael. Go-alaynu Adonoi tzva-ot sh'mo, kedosh Yisrael. Baruch Ata Adonoi, ga-al Yisrael.*

***Rock*** *of Israel, arise and help Israel; redeem, as You said, Judah and Israel. Our redeemer is the God of Hosts — that is His name — and the holy One of Israel. Blessed are You, God, redeemer of Israel.*

"Rock of Israel." That's what we call You. You are our rock in good times and bad. You come to our aid in each generation — that's the only reason we're still here. You promised never to let us fall through the cracks, and You sure kept Your word. I bless You today, God, Who redeemed us nationally then, and Who continues to do so, today and always.

# Amidah

*The Amidah is the centerpiece of the daily prayers. It literally means "standing," as it is recited while standing. It consists of nineteen specific blessings, and covers every basic need known to man. The Amidah should be said at a time and place where a person will not be disturbed. One should not interrupt to speak of other things in the middle of any prayer — but this is especially true of the Amidah. While praying the Amidah, one should face east, toward Israel (or whichever direction is toward Israel for the one praying). One should stand with feet together and not move the feet until completion. One should try to truly envision standing before our kind and benevolent God, Who is just waiting to hear from us. One should pray the Amidah in a whisper or undertone. This is between you and God.*

*Daily Prayers* 59

אֲדֹנָי שְׂפָתַי תִּפְתָּח וּפִי יַגִּיד תְּהִלָּתֶךָ.

**Adonoi** *s'fa-tai tiftach, u-fi yagid tehilatecha.*

**My** Lord, open my lips, and may my mouth speak Your praises.

Dear God,

I stand here before You, ready to share my thoughts and reflections with You. It's intimidating, and I don't want to do it wrong! But I'm just going to start... I know You'll understand.

## ANCESTORS

*Bow at the beginning and end of this blessing.*

בָּרוּךְ אַתָּה יְיָ אֱלֹהֵינוּ וֵאלֹהֵי אֲבוֹתֵינוּ, אֱלֹהֵי אַבְרָהָם, אֱלֹהֵי יִצְחָק, וֵאלֹהֵי יַעֲקֹב, הָאֵל הַגָּדוֹל הַגִּבּוֹר וְהַנּוֹרָא, אֵל עֶלְיוֹן, גּוֹמֵל חֲסָדִים טוֹבִים, וְקוֹנֵה הַכֹּל, וְזוֹכֵר חַסְדֵי אָבוֹת, וּמֵבִיא גוֹאֵל לִבְנֵי בְנֵיהֶם, לְמַעַן שְׁמוֹ בְּאַהֲבָה. מֶלֶךְ עוֹזֵר וּמוֹשִׁיעַ וּמָגֵן. בָּרוּךְ אַתָּה יְיָ, מָגֵן אַבְרָהָם.

**Baruch** *Ata Adonoi, Elohaynu vay-lohay avotaynu, Elohay Avraham, Elohay Yitzchok, vay-lohay Yaakov. Ha-El ha-gadol ha-gibor v'ha-nora El elyon, go-mel chasadim tovim, v'konay ha-kol, v'zocher chasday avot, u-may-vi go-el liv-nay v'nayhem, l'ma-an sh'mo b'ahava. Melech ozer u-moshiya u-magen. Baruch Ata Adonoi, magen Avraham.*

**Blessed** are You, God, our God, and the God of our ancestors, God of Abraham, God of Isaac, God of Jacob. The great, strong, and awesome God; exalted God, Who bestows good kindnesses, owns everything, remembers the kindness of our ancestors, and brings a redeemer to their grandchildren, for the sake of His name, with love. King, helper, savior, and shield. Blessed are You, God, shield of Abraham.

The first thing I'd like to do, God, is acknowledge that while I think I'm a pretty good person overall, I do often forget that You are the source of everything in my life. Fortunately, God, I have our Jewish role models, Abraham, Isaac, and Jacob, who came before us, who did not take that gift for granted. They were so loyal to You, and please remember on this important day that I am one of their children. Be kind to me for their sakes — if not for my own.

## GOD'S STRENGTH

אַתָּה גִּבּוֹר לְעוֹלָם אֲדֹנָי, מְחַיֶּה מֵתִים אַתָּה, רַב לְהוֹשִׁיעַ. (בחורף: מַשִּׁיב הָרוּחַ וּמוֹרִיד הַגֶּשֶׁם.) מְכַלְכֵּל חַיִּים בְּחֶסֶד, מְחַיֶּה מֵתִים בְּרַחֲמִים רַבִּים, סוֹמֵךְ נוֹפְלִים, וְרוֹפֵא חוֹלִים, וּמַתִּיר אֲסוּרִים, וּמְקַיֵּם אֱמוּנָתוֹ לִישֵׁנֵי עָפָר, מִי כָמוֹךָ בַּעַל גְּבוּרוֹת וּמִי דּוֹמֶה לָּךְ, מֶלֶךְ מֵמִית וּמְחַיֶּה וּמַצְמִיחַ יְשׁוּעָה. וְנֶאֱמָן אַתָּה לְהַחֲיוֹת מֵתִים. בָּרוּךְ אַתָּה יְיָ, מְחַיֶּה הַמֵּתִים.

***Ata*** *gibor l'olam Adonoi, mechayeh may-tim Ata rav l'hoshiya.* **[In winter: *Mashiv ha-ruach u-morid ha-gashem.*]** *Mechalkel chaim b'chesed, m'chayeh maytim b'rachamim rabim. Somech noflim v'rofay cholim, u-matir asurim, u-m'kayem emunato li-shaynay afar. Mi chamocha ba-al gevurot u-mi domeh lach, melech may-mit u-m'chayeh, u-matz-miyach yeshua. V'ne-eman Ata l'hachayot may-tim. Baruch Ata Adonoi, m'chayeh ha-maytim.*

Daily Prayers

***You*** *are eternally strong, God. You revive the dead and save abundantly.* **[In winter: You blow the wind and bring down the rain.]** *You sustain the living ones with kindness, You revive the dead with great compassion. You support the fallen, heal the sick, release the bound, and keep Your promise to those that are already resting in the dust. Who is like You, master of strengths? Who can compare to You? You are the King Who brings death and restores life and plants the seeds of redemption. You are trustworthy to revive the dead. Blessed are You, God, Who revives the dead.*

God, I acknowledge that You are the source of life and death. Sometimes we get distracted by all the other "causes" — but I affirm that life and death are in Your hands. No one else has that power.

## HOLINESS

אַתָּה קָדוֹשׁ וְשִׁמְךָ קָדוֹשׁ, וּקְדוֹשִׁים בְּכָל יוֹם יְהַלְלוּךָ סֶּלָה.
בָּרוּךְ אַתָּה יְיָ, הָאֵל הַקָּדוֹשׁ.

***Ata*** *kadosh v'shimcha kadosh u-kedoshim b'chol yom y'halelucha selah. Baruch Ata Adonoi, ha-El ha-kadosh.*

***You*** *are holy and Your name is holy, and holy ones praise You daily. Blessed are You, God, the holy God.*

God, as I stand here before You, I need to take a minute to focus on Who You actually are. How is it that the most powerful Being in the world is available to me, 24/7? You handle the weather. You keep us alive every day. You are so compassionate. You support me when I fall. You heal the sick. And You keep Your promises to those that are long gone. Who else is like that? And although I am not so well-versed in "holiness," God, if anyone is holy, it's You. Sometimes I meet people, or places that feel "holy" — it's because they contain a spark of You. You are the source of that.

---

HOW IS IT THAT THE MOST POWERFUL BEING IN THE WORLD IS AVAILABLE TO ME, 24/7?

---

## WISDOM

אַתָּה חוֹנֵן לְאָדָם דַּעַת, וּמְלַמֵּד לֶאֱנוֹשׁ בִּינָה. חָנֵּנוּ מֵאִתְּךָ דֵּעָה, בִּינָה וְהַשְׂכֵּל. בָּרוּךְ אַתָּה יְיָ, חוֹנֵן הַדָּעַת.

***Ata*** *chonen l'adam da-at u-m'lamed le-enosh bina. Chanaynu may-itcha day-a bina v'haskel. Baruch Ata Adonoi, chonen ha-da-at.*

**You** *have gifted humans with wisdom, and have taught insight to mortal man. Grace us with wisdom, insight, and understanding from You. Blessed are You, God, Who graces us with wisdom.*

God, please gift me with wisdom to make good choices and good judgments. You are the wisest Being that ever was, and the source of all wisdom is You, so please… share some of that wisdom with me and with my loved ones. In my daily interactions, help me to be perceptive, intuitive, and eloquent. Thank You!

## REPENTANCE & FORGIVENESS

הֲשִׁיבֵנוּ אָבִינוּ לְתוֹרָתֶךָ, וְקָרְבֵנוּ מַלְכֵּנוּ לַעֲבוֹדָתֶךָ, וְהַחֲזִירֵנוּ בִּתְשׁוּבָה שְׁלֵמָה לְפָנֶיךָ. בָּרוּךְ אַתָּה יְיָ, הָרוֹצֶה בִּתְשׁוּבָה.

**סְלַח** לָנוּ, אָבִינוּ, כִּי חָטָאנוּ, מְחַל לָנוּ, מַלְכֵּנוּ, כִּי פָשָׁעְנוּ, כִּי מוֹחֵל וְסוֹלֵחַ אָתָּה. בָּרוּךְ אַתָּה יְיָ, חַנּוּן הַמַּרְבֶּה לִסְלֹחַ.

*Gently thump your chest with your fist at the words "chatanu" and "fashanu" — "we have sinned" and "we have erred" — to indicate that mistakes originate in the heart.*

**Hashivaynu** avinu l'Torah-techa, v'karvaynu malkaynu la-avodatecha, v'hacha-ziraynu bi-teshuva she-layma l'fanecha. Baruch Ata Adonoi, ha-rotzeh bi-teshuva.

**Slach** lanu avinu ki chatanu. Mechal lanu malkaynu ki fashanu. Ki mochel v'solayach Ata. Baruch Ata Adonoi, chanun ha-marbeh li-slo-ach.

**Return** us, our Father, to Your Torah, and bring us near, our King, to Your service, and bring us back in full repentance before You. Blessed are You, God, Who desired our repentance.

**Forgive** us, our Father, for we have sinned. Absolve us, our King, for we have erred. For You are forgiving and absolving. Blessed are You, God, compassionate One, Who forgives abundantly.

God, help me to be the best Jew that I can be. While everyone makes mistakes, don't let me drift too far from my best self. I don't want to drift from You, and be distant from my spiritual source. Give me inspiration and role models. Forgive me when I goof.

(Specifically, God, forgive me for _____. I sincerely commit to never do it again, with Your help.) I know that You are a compassionate and forgiving God, and I am grateful for the gift of repentance and forgiveness.

## FEEL OUR PAIN

רְאֵה בְעָנְיֵנוּ, וְרִיבָה רִיבֵנוּ, וּגְאָלֵנוּ מְהֵרָה לְמַעַן שְׁמֶךָ, כִּי גּוֹאֵל חָזָק אָתָּה. בָּרוּךְ אַתָּה יְיָ, גּוֹאֵל יִשְׂרָאֵל.

**R'ay** *v'an-yaynu v'riva ri-vaynu u-g'alaynu m'hayra l'ma-an sh'mecha, ki go-el chazak Ata. Baruch Ata Adonoi, go-el Yisrael.*

**See** *our pain, and fight our fight, and redeem us soon, for the sake of Your Name, for You are a mighty redeemer. Blessed are You, God, redeemer of Israel.*

God, there are so many things in life that are painful. Some are personal, like difficult relationships, or life's circumstances that feel so hard. Some are more global, like the state of the Jewish people, anti-semitism, and hatred of Israel. But You, God, have the power to see our pain — whether personal or global — and fight our fight. Please, God, take us out of our painful realities, and bring us to a state of peace, harmony, and serenity.

## HEALING

רְפָאֵנוּ, יְיָ, וְנֵרָפֵא, הוֹשִׁיעֵנוּ וְנִוָּשֵׁעָה, כִּי תְהִלָּתֵנוּ אָתָּה, וְהַעֲלֵה רְפוּאָה שְׁלֵמָה לְכָל מַכּוֹתֵינוּ. כִּי אֵל מֶלֶךְ רוֹפֵא נֶאֱמָן וְרַחֲמָן אָתָּה. בָּרוּךְ אַתָּה יְיָ, רוֹפֵא חוֹלֵי עַמּוֹ יִשְׂרָאֵל.

**Refa-aynu** *Adonoi v'nay-rafay, hoshi-aynu v'niva-shaya, ki tehila-taynu Ata. V'ha-alay refuah shelayma l'chol makotaynu.*

**Optional prayer for a specific person who needs healing:**
*Yehi ratzon mil-fanecha Adonoi Elohai vay-lohay avotai she-tishlach refuah shelayma min ha-shamayim, refuat ha-nefesh u-refuat ha-guf*

*Daily Prayers* 65

**for a male:** *la-choleh*

**for a female:** *la-cholah*

**[Insert name of ill person with the formula (Hebrew name) ben/bat (mother's Hebrew name)]**

*b'toch sh'ar cholay Yisrael.*

**Ki** *El melech rofay ne-eman v'rachaman Ata. Baruch Ata Adonoi, rofay cholay amo Yisrael.*

**Heal** us, God, and we will be healed. Save us, and we'll be saved, for You are our praise. And bring a complete recovery for all of our ills.

**Optional prayer for a specific person who needs healing:**
*May it be Your will before You, God, our God, and the God of our ancestors, that You send a complete recovery from heaven, a healing of the body and a healing of the spirit, to the following sick person:*

**[Insert name of ill person with the formula (Hebrew name) son/daughter of (mother's Hebrew name)]:**
*among all the other ill people of Israel.*

**For** You are a healing God and King Who is faithful and compassionate. Blessed are You, God, Who heals the sick people of Israel.

God, there are so many people who are ill. Young people, old people, even children. It's so hard to understand, God! It's so hard to watch people suffer! There's cancer, mental illness, and all kinds of physical and psychological disorders. You, God, have the power to send healing and recovery. Please, God, see our pain and suffering and bring healing to all Your people who need it.

**Optional:**

Specifically, God, please heal and bring recovery, quickly and easily, to [insert name of ill person with the formula (Hebrew name) ben/bat (mother's Hebrew name)]. Help him/her to regain all his/her capacities, whether physical, mental, or emotional. Allow him/her to grow old in joy and health, and be able to enjoy all that life has to offer, and to reach his/her potential, together with all of the rest of our nation.

You are the most compassionate and powerful being, God, so please, help us to recover from all the sickness and pain, and keep us healthy till 120.

## MAKING A LIVING

בָּרֵךְ עָלֵינוּ, יְיָ אֱלֹהֵינוּ, אֶת הַשָּׁנָה הַזֹּאת וְאֶת כָּל מִינֵי תְבוּאָתָהּ לְטוֹבָה,

(בַּקַּיִץ) וְתֵן בְּרָכָה (בַּחֹרֶף) וְתֵן טַל וּמָטָר לִבְרָכָה

עַל פְּנֵי הָאֲדָמָה, וְשַׂבְּעֵנוּ מִטּוּבֶךָ, וּבָרֵךְ שְׁנָתֵנוּ כַּשָּׁנִים הַטּוֹבוֹת. בָּרוּךְ אַתָּה יְיָ, מְבָרֵךְ הַשָּׁנִים.

**Barech** *alaynu Adonoi Elohaynu et ha-shana ha-zot v'et kol minay tevu-ata l'tova, v'ten*

**in summer**: *bracha*

**in winter**: *tal u-matar li-vracha*

*al p'nay ha-adama v'sabaynu mi-tuvecha. U-varech shna-taynu ka-shanim ha-tovot. Baruch Ata Adonoi, mevarech ha-shanim.*

**Send** blessing upon us, God, our God, for this year, and for all the species of crops for the good. And send

**in summer**: blessing

**in winter**: dew and rain for blessing

on the face of the earth, and let us be satisfied from Your goodness. And bless our years like the best of years. Blessed are You, God, who blesses the years.

God, let's face it. Financially, there are good years and bad years. Sometimes it seems so unexpected — a new client just materializes right when we need it, or conversely, we do everything right and the economy tanks. God, think of the best year I ever had, and bless me with another year just like that. Because I really need Your blessing, God, so that I can support myself [and my family] with dignity and pride, and not be harried, hassled, and stressed financially. I'm asking for Your blessing to pay the bills, and be able to live a good life with those I love. And God, when the blessings do come, please let me remember that it's all from You, and to be grateful. Please keep in mind the following people who could use some help making a living or finding a job: **[mention their names here].**

BRING US BACK

**תְּקַע** בְּשׁוֹפָר גָּדוֹל לְחֵרוּתֵנוּ, וְשָׂא נֵס לְקַבֵּץ גָּלֻיּוֹתֵינוּ, וְקַבְּצֵנוּ יַחַד מֵאַרְבַּע כַּנְפוֹת הָאָרֶץ. בָּרוּךְ אַתָּה יְיָ, מְקַבֵּץ נִדְחֵי עַמּוֹ יִשְׂרָאֵל.

**T'ka** *b'shofar gadol l'chay-rutaynu, v'sa nes l'kabetz galuyotaynu, v'kab-tzaynu yachad may-arba kanfot ha-aretz. Baruch Ata Adonoi, m'kabetz nid-chay amo Yisrael.*

**Blow** *the great shofar for our redemption, and lift the flag of the ingathering of the exiles, and gather together all of us from the four corners of the earth. Blessed are You, God, Who gathers the far-flung ones of His nation Israel.*

God, our nation, the Jewish people, is so dispersed. We are dispersed geographically and spiritually. Although we are all brothers and sisters, we are so far from feeling that unity, and many of us are confused and disparate about our identity as Jews. Back in the day, we all lived in the Land of Israel, with a clear purpose and mission. I wish that we could reclaim that unity, that mission, that purpose. I wish we had peace and connection with each other and with You. Gather us together once again, God, to be Your nation in unison.

## CLARITY

הָשִׁיבָה שׁוֹפְטֵינוּ כְּבָרִאשׁוֹנָה וְיוֹעֲצֵינוּ כְּבַתְּחִלָּה, וְהָסֵר מִמֶּנּוּ יָגוֹן וַאֲנָחָה, וּמְלוֹךְ עָלֵינוּ אַתָּה, יְיָ, לְבַדְּךָ בְּחֶסֶד וּבְרַחֲמִים, וְצַדְּקֵנוּ בַּמִּשְׁפָּט. בָּרוּךְ אַתָּה יְיָ, מֶלֶךְ אוֹהֵב צְדָקָה וּמִשְׁפָּט (בעשי״ת הַמֶּלֶךְ הַמִּשְׁפָּט).

**Hashiva** *shof-taynu k'varishona, v'yo-atzaynu k'vat-chila, v'haser mi-menu yagon va-anacha, u-m'loch alaynu Ata Adonoi l'vadcha b'chesed u-v'rachamim. V'tzad-kaynu ba-mishpat. Baruch Ata Adonoi, melech ohev tzedaka u-mishpat.*

**Return** *our judges as in the beginning, and our advisors as it used to be, and remove from us agony and anguish, and reign over us, You, our God, alone, with kindness and compassion. And vindicate us in judgment. Blessed are You, God, King Who loves charity and justice.*

God, in the days of old, in the Land of Israel, when we had our Holy Temple standing at our center in Jerusalem, we had such incredible clarity. If we had pain, anguish, or agony, we would turn to our prophets and spiritual judges to clear the way for us, show us what was right, and teach

Daily Prayers   69

us what to do. Please, bring back that clarity! Take away our pain and agony! Judge us righteously and fairly, and be good to us!

## TAKE CARE OF THE BAD PEOPLE

**וְלַמַּלְשִׁינִים** אַל תְּהִי תִקְוָה, וְכָל הָרִשְׁעָה כְּרֶגַע תֹּאבֵד, וְכָל אוֹיְבֶיךָ מְהֵרָה יִכָּרֵתוּ, וְהַזֵּדִים מְהֵרָה תְעַקֵּר וּתְשַׁבֵּר וּתְמַגֵּר וְתַכְנִיעַ בִּמְהֵרָה בְיָמֵינוּ. בָּרוּךְ אַתָּה יְיָ, שֹׁבֵר אֹיְבִים וּמַכְנִיעַ זֵדִים.

**V'lamal-shinim** al te-hi tikva, v'chol ha-risha k'rega to-ved, v'chol oy-vecha m'hayra yi-karaytu, v'hazaydim m'hayra t'aker u-t'shaber, u-t'mager v'tachniya bim-hayra v'yamaynu. Baruch Ata Adonoi, shover oy-vim u-mach-niya zaydim.

**And** for the informers [Jewish turncoats who turned fellow Jews in to the non-Jewish enemies], may there be no hope, and may all the evil be gone in a moment, and may all Your enemies quickly be cut down, and may the sinners quickly be uprooted, broken, finished, and humbled, quickly and in our days. Blessed are You, God, Who breaks the enemies and humbles arrogant sinners.

God, we look around the world, and we see all kinds of evil. We can't necessarily take it into our hands to overpower all this evil. So we pray to You to deal with all those who desire our downfall. I won't be violent to them, nor do I always see that bad people get what they deserve — but I trust that You, God, right all the wrongs, and eventually bring justice to the world, by punishing evil to the fullest extent possible.

## TAKE CARE OF THE GOOD PEOPLE

עַל הַצַּדִּיקִים וְעַל הַחֲסִידִים וְעַל זִקְנֵי עַמְּךָ בֵּית יִשְׂרָאֵל, וְעַל פְּלֵיטַת סוֹפְרֵיהֶם, וְעַל גֵּרֵי הַצֶּדֶק וְעָלֵינוּ, יֶהֱמוּ נָא רַחֲמֶיךָ, יְיָ אֱלֹהֵינוּ, וְתֵן שָׂכָר טוֹב לְכָל הַבּוֹטְחִים בְּשִׁמְךָ בֶּאֱמֶת, וְשִׂים חֶלְקֵנוּ עִמָּהֶם לְעוֹלָם, וְלֹא נֵבוֹשׁ כִּי בְךָ בָּטָחְנוּ. בָּרוּךְ אַתָּה יְיָ, מִשְׁעָן וּמִבְטָח לַצַּדִּיקִים.

***Al*** *ha-tzadikim v'al ha-chasidim, v'al zik-nay amcha bayt Yisrael, v'al play-tat sof-rayhem, v'al gayray ha-tzedek v'alaynu. Yehemu na rachamecha Adonoi Elohaynu. V'tayn sachar tov l'chol ha-bot-chim b'shimcha be-emet. V'sim chel-kaynu imahem l'olam, v'lo nay-vosh ki b'cha batachnu. Baruch Ata Adonoi, mishan u-mivtach la-tzadikim.*

**May** Your mercy be aroused, God, our God, on the righteous people, on the devout, on the elders of the house of Your nation Israel, on the remnant of their scribes, on the righteous converts, and on us. Give a good reward to all who trust in Your name in truth. And put our lot with theirs forever, and may we not feel ashamed — because we trust in You. Blessed are You, God, support and trust of the righteous.

God, sometimes it seems as though the bad people have it good, and the good guys get overlooked, ignored, and stepped on. Please pay special attention to those good eggs — the ones who do the right thing, trust in You, are kind to others, and have sacrificed to be Jewish. Be good to them, and don't let them get pushed aside by the louder and brasher elements. Remember them, and us with them, and don't let them, or us, ever feel embarrassed by our faith and devotion to You.

---

*GOD, SOMETIMES IT SEEMS AS THOUGH THE BAD PEOPLE HAVE IT GOOD, AND THE GOOD GUYS GET OVERLOOKED, IGNORED, AND STEPPED ON.*

---

## JERUSALEM & KING DAVID

**וְלִירוּשָׁלַיִם** עִירְךָ בְּרַחֲמִים תָּשׁוּב, וְתִשְׁכּוֹן בְּתוֹכָהּ כַּאֲשֶׁר דִּבַּרְתָּ, וּבְנֵה אוֹתָהּ בְּקָרוֹב בְּיָמֵינוּ בִּנְיַן עוֹלָם, וְכִסֵּא דָוִד מְהֵרָה לְתוֹכָהּ תָּכִין. בָּרוּךְ אַתָּה יְיָ, בּוֹנֵה יְרוּשָׁלָיִם.

**אֶת** צֶמַח דָּוִד עַבְדְּךָ מְהֵרָה תַצְמִיחַ, וְקַרְנוֹ תָּרוּם בִּישׁוּעָתֶךָ, כִּי לִישׁוּעָתְךָ קִוִּינוּ כָּל הַיּוֹם. בָּרוּךְ אַתָּה יְיָ, מַצְמִיחַ קֶרֶן יְשׁוּעָה.

**V'li-Yerushalayim** ircha b'rachamim tashuv. V'tishkon b'tocha ka-asher di-barta. U-vnay ota b'karov b'yamaynu binyan olam. V'kisay David m'hayra l'tocha tachin. Baruch Ata Adonoi, bonay Yerushalayim.

**Et** tzemach David avd'cha m'hayra tatz-miyach. V'karno tarum bi-yeshu-a-techa, ki li-yeshu-atcha kivinu kol hayom. Baruch Ata Adonoi, matz-mi-ach keren yeshu-a.

**And** to Your city, Jerusalem, return in compassion, and dwell in it as You have spoken. And build it, soon, in our days — an everlasting structure. And may the throne of David, our king, be quickly established in it. Blessed are You, God, Who builds Jerusalem.

**May** You grow the seed of David, Your servant, quickly! And raise his horn in Your salvation, because we wait all day for Your salvation. Blessed are You, God, Who makes the ray of salvation grow.

God, Israel is that special epicenter of Judaism, and Jerusalem is the crux of that epicenter. Almost every Jew feels connected to it, even if he's never been there. I pray for the day, God, that there will be a peaceful, spiritual, and complete restoration of Jerusalem to once again become that epicenter, with King David at the helm, leading us in kindness, justice, and peace.

## HEAR OUR PRAYERS

שְׁמַע קוֹלֵנוּ, יְיָ אֱלֹהֵינוּ, חוּס וְרַחֵם עָלֵינוּ, וְקַבֵּל בְּרַחֲמִים וּבְרָצוֹן אֶת תְּפִלָּתֵנוּ, כִּי אֵל שׁוֹמֵעַ תְּפִלּוֹת וְתַחֲנוּנִים אָתָּה, וּמִלְּפָנֶיךָ, מַלְכֵּנוּ, רֵיקָם אַל תְּשִׁיבֵנוּ. כִּי אַתָּה שׁוֹמֵעַ תְּפִלַּת עַמְּךָ יִשְׂרָאֵל בְּרַחֲמִים. בָּרוּךְ אַתָּה יְיָ, שׁוֹמֵעַ תְּפִלָּה.

**Shema** *kolaynu, Adonoi Elohaynu, chus v'rachem alaynu, v'kabel b'rachamim u-v'ratzon et tefilataynu. Ki El shomaya tefilot v'tachanunim Ata. U-mil-fanecha malkaynu ray-kam al t'shi-vaynu.* [Insert, in your own words, any personal requests.] *Ki Ata shomaya tefilat amcha Yisrael b'rachamim. Baruch Ata Adonoi, shomaya tefilah.*

**Hear** *our voices, God, our God. Have mercy and compassion on us, and accept our prayers with compassion and willingness. For You are God, Who listens to our prayers and entreaties. And, our King, don't send us from before You empty-handed.* [Insert, in your own words, any personal requests.] *For You listen to the prayers of Your nation Israel with compassion. Blessed are You, God, Who listens to prayers.*

God, hear me. Accept and internalize my words. Have compassion on me. I know You hear everything I say. Here are some other things that are on my mind *[Insert, in your own words, any personal requests]*. I know You are listening, and that You care. Thank You!

*Daily Prayers*

## ACCEPT OUR PRAYERS

רְצֵה, יְיָ אֱלֹהֵינוּ, בְּעַמְּךָ יִשְׂרָאֵל וּבִתְפִלָּתָם, וְהָשֵׁב אֶת הָעֲבוֹדָה לִדְבִיר בֵּיתֶךָ, וְאִשֵּׁי יִשְׂרָאֵל, וּתְפִלָּתָם בְּאַהֲבָה תְקַבֵּל בְּרָצוֹן, וּתְהִי לְרָצוֹן תָּמִיד עֲבוֹדַת יִשְׂרָאֵל עַמֶּךָ

וְתֶחֱזֶינָה עֵינֵינוּ בְּשׁוּבְךָ לְצִיּוֹן בְּרַחֲמִים. בָּרוּךְ אַתָּה יְיָ, הַמַּחֲזִיר שְׁכִינָתוֹ לְצִיּוֹן.

**R'tzay** Adonoi Elohaynu b'amcha Yisrael u-vi-tefilatam, v'hashev et ha-avodah li-dvir bay-techa. V'ishay Yisrael u-tefilatam, b'ahava tekabel b'ratzon, u-tehi l'ratzon tamid avodat Yisrael amecha. V'techezena aynaynu b'shuvcha l'tziyon b'rachamim. Baruch Ata Adonoi, ha-machazir shechi-nato l'tziyon.

**God,** our God, desire Your nation Israel, and their prayers, and restore the temple service to the sanctuary of Your home. Accept with love and willingness the offerings and prayers of the Jewish people, and may the service of Your nation Israel always be favorable to You. May our eyes see Your return to Zion with compassion. Blessed are You, God, Who restores His holy presence to Zion.

God, back in Temple times, we could talk to You with our belongings. We would offer You our possessions, and see that You'd accepted them. Now, life is far more ambiguous. I stand here and offer You my innermost yearnings, and just pray that they are accepted. As I come toward the end of the Amidah, I ask: please accept my words in the manner that they're offered — in earnestness, sincerity, and honesty. And one day, maybe I'll be able to visit the Temple again, and see that miracle of acceptance with my own eyes.

---
I STAND HERE AND OFFER YOU MY INNERMOST YEARNINGS,
AND JUST PRAY THAT THEY ARE ACCEPTED.
---

## GRATITUDE

*Bow at the beginning and end of this prayer.*

מוֹדִים אֲנַחְנוּ לָךְ, שָׁאַתָּה הוּא, יְיָ אֱלֹהֵינוּ וֵאלֹהֵי אֲבוֹתֵינוּ, לְעוֹלָם וָעֶד, צוּר חַיֵּינוּ, מָגֵן יִשְׁעֵנוּ, אַתָּה הוּא לְדוֹר וָדוֹר, נוֹדֶה לְךָ וּנְסַפֵּר תְּהִלָּתֶךָ, עַל חַיֵּינוּ הַמְּסוּרִים בְּיָדֶךָ, וְעַל נִשְׁמוֹתֵינוּ הַפְּקוּדוֹת לָךְ, וְעַל נִסֶּיךָ שֶׁבְּכָל יוֹם עִמָּנוּ, וְעַל נִפְלְאוֹתֶיךָ וְטוֹבוֹתֶיךָ שֶׁבְּכָל עֵת, עֶרֶב וָבֹקֶר וְצָהֳרָיִם, הַטּוֹב, כִּי לֹא כָלוּ רַחֲמֶיךָ, וְהַמְרַחֵם, כִּי לֹא תַמּוּ חֲסָדֶיךָ, מֵעוֹלָם קִוִּינוּ לָךְ.

וְעַל כֻּלָּם יִתְבָּרַךְ וְיִתְרוֹמַם שִׁמְךָ מַלְכֵּנוּ תָּמִיד לְעוֹלָם וָעֶד. וְכֹל הַחַיִּים יוֹדוּךָ סֶּלָה, וִיהַלְלוּ אֶת שִׁמְךָ בֶּאֱמֶת, הָאֵל יְשׁוּעָתֵנוּ וְעֶזְרָתֵנוּ סֶלָה. בָּרוּךְ אַתָּה יְיָ, הַטּוֹב שִׁמְךָ וּלְךָ נָאֶה לְהוֹדוֹת.

**Modim** anachnu lach, she-Ata hu Adonoi Elohaynu vay-lohay avotaynu, l'olam va-ed. Tzur chai-aynu, magen yish-aynu Ata hu l'dor va-dor. Nodeh l'cha u-nesaper tehilatecha al chai-aynu ha-mesurim b'yadecha v'al nish-motaynu ha-pekudot lach, v'al nisecha she-b'chol yom imanu, v'al nifle-otecha v'tovotecha, she-b'chol ayt, erev va-voker v'tzaharayim. Ha-tov ki lo chalu rachamecha, v'ha-merachem ki lo tamu chasadecha, may-olam kivinu lach.

**V'al** kulam yit-barach v'yit-romam v'yit-nasay shimcha malkaynu tamid l'olam va-ed. V'chol ha-chaim yoducha selah, vi-hallelu et shimcha be-emet, ha-El

*Daily Prayers*

*yeshu-ataynu v'ezrataynu selah. Baruch Ata Adonoi, ha-tov shimcha u-l'cha na-eh l'hodot.*

**We** give thanks before You, that You are God, our God, and the God of our ancestors, forever. You are the Rock of our lives, the Shield of our salvation, from generation to generation. We will thank You, and tell the story of Your praise, about our lives, which are entrusted to Your hands, and about our souls, which are safeguarded with You, and about Your miracles which are with us every day, and about Your wonders and good deeds, that are with us always — evening, morning, and afternoon. You are good, because Your compassion never ends, and You are compassionate, because Your kindnesses never cease. May we always hope to You.

**And** for all of these, may Your name be blessed, exalted, elevated, our God, always and forever. And may all the living thank You, forever, and praise Your name in truth, oh, God, our salvation and our helper, forever. Blessed are You, God, Whose name is good, and to You it is fitting to thank.

God, I sincerely want to say thank You. For being our God. For being our Rock. For our lives, that are dependent on You. For our souls, that are a spark of You. For Your small miracles that are with us every day. For the good things You do for us every moment of every day. Your compassion never runs out! Your kindnesses never stop! "Thank you" almost seems pathetic. But it's the best I've got, God. For all these, God, I hope humans always recognize Your greatness. And I, for one, will do my share and resolve to be more grateful.

## PEACE

**שִׂים** שָׁלוֹם טוֹבָה וּבְרָכָה, חֵן וָחֶסֶד וְרַחֲמִים, עָלֵינוּ וְעַל כָּל יִשְׂרָאֵל עַמֶּךָ. בָּרְכֵנוּ, אָבִינוּ, כֻּלָּנוּ כְּאֶחָד בְּאוֹר פָּנֶיךָ, כִּי בְאוֹר פָּנֶיךָ נָתַתָּ לָּנוּ, יְיָ אֱלֹהֵינוּ, תּוֹרַת חַיִּים וְאַהֲבַת חֶסֶד, וּצְדָקָה וּבְרָכָה וְרַחֲמִים וְחַיִּים וְשָׁלוֹם, וְטוֹב בְּעֵינֶיךָ לְבָרֵךְ אֶת עַמְּךָ יִשְׂרָאֵל בְּכָל עֵת וּבְכָל שָׁעָה בִּשְׁלוֹמֶךָ.

**בָּרוּךְ** אַתָּה יְיָ, הַמְבָרֵךְ אֶת עַמּוֹ יִשְׂרָאֵל בַּשָּׁלוֹם.

**Sim** *shalom tova u-vracha chayn va-chesed v'rachamim, alaynu v'al kol Yisrael amecha, barchaynu avinu kulanu k'echad b'or panecha, ki v'or panecha natata lanu Adonoi Elohaynu torat chaim v'ahavat chesed, u-tzedaka u-vracha v'rachamim v'chaim v'shalom v'tov b'aynecha l'varech et amcha Yisrael b'chol ayt u-v'chol sha-ah bi-shlomecha. Baruch Ata Adonoi, ha-mevarech et amo Yisrael ba-shalom.*

**Establish** peace, goodness, blessing, grace, kindness, and compassion on us and on all of Israel, Your nation. Bless us, our Father, all of us as one, with the light of Your face, for with the light of Your face You've given us — God, our God — a Torah of life, love of kindness, charity, blessing, compassion, life, peace, and goodness. May it be good in Your eyes to bless all of Your nation Israel, at all times and in every moment, with Your peace. Blessed are You, God, Who blesses His nation Israel with peace.

God, please help our world to be more peaceful. I pray not just for peace, but for lots of other things that go along with it: goodness, blessing, life,

*Daily Prayers*

mutual respect, kindness, compassion. Bless us with Your special, peaceful light — that "holiness" that I mentioned earlier. It was that light with which You gifted us the Torah. It hurts me so much that Jewish people misunderstand each other so badly and that there is so much horrible infighting. I imagine it must pain You too, God. Please: bless Your people Israel, always, with peace.

## CONCLUSION

אֱלֹהַי, נְצוֹר לְשׁוֹנִי מֵרָע, וּשְׂפָתַי מִדַּבֵּר מִרְמָה, וְלִמְקַלְלַי נַפְשִׁי תִדֹּם, וְנַפְשִׁי כֶּעָפָר לַכֹּל תִּהְיֶה. פְּתַח לִבִּי בְּתוֹרָתֶךָ, וּבְמִצְוֹתֶיךָ תִּרְדּוֹף נַפְשִׁי. וְכָל הַחוֹשְׁבִים עָלַי רָעָה, מְהֵרָה הָפֵר עֲצָתָם וְקַלְקֵל מַחֲשַׁבְתָּם. עֲשֵׂה לְמַעַן שְׁמֶךָ, עֲשֵׂה לְמַעַן יְמִינֶךָ, עֲשֵׂה לְמַעַן קְדֻשָּׁתֶךָ, עֲשֵׂה לְמַעַן תּוֹרָתֶךָ. לְמַעַן יֵחָלְצוּן יְדִידֶיךָ, הוֹשִׁיעָה יְמִינְךָ וַעֲנֵנִי. יִהְיוּ לְרָצוֹן אִמְרֵי פִי וְהֶגְיוֹן לִבִּי לְפָנֶיךָ, יְיָ צוּרִי וְגוֹאֲלִי. עֹשֶׂה שָׁלוֹם בִּמְרוֹמָיו, הוּא יַעֲשֶׂה שָׁלוֹם עָלֵינוּ, וְעַל כָּל יִשְׂרָאֵל, וְאִמְרוּ אָמֵן.

**Elohai,** *netzor l'shoni mayra u-sefatai mi-daber mirma. V'lim-ka-lelai nafshi tidom, v'nafshi ke-afar lakol ti-hiyeh. P'tach libi b'Torah-techa u-v'mitzvotecha tirdof nafshi, v'chol ha-choshvim alai ra-ah m'hayra ha-fayr atzatam v'kalkel macha-shavtam. Asay l'ma-an sh'mecha, asay l'ma-an y'minecha, asay l'ma-an k'dusha-techa, asay l'ma-an Torah-techa. L'ma-an yay-chal-tzun y'didecha, ho-shiya yemincha va-anayni. Yi-hiyu l'ratzon imray fi, v'heg-yon libi l'fanecha, Adonoi tzuri v'go-ali.*

**My** *God. Restrain my tongue from bad, and my lips from speaking deceitfully. May my soul be silent when others* curse me, and may my essence be like dust to all. Open my heart in Your Torah and may my soul pursue Your mitzvot. May all those who wish evil for me have their plots quickly nullified and their plans ruined. Do it for Your name, do it for Your right hand, do it for Your holiness, do it for Your Torah. Save Your right hand and answer me so that Your dear ones may rest. May the words of my mouth and the thoughts of my heart be favorable before You, God, my Rock and Redeemer.

*Take three steps backward to symbolize moving out of the immediate company of God.*
*Bow left and say: Oseh shalom bi-mromav*
*Bow right and say: Hu ya-aseh shalom alaynu*
*Bow forward and say: V'al kol Yisrael*
*Straighten up and say: V'imru amen.*

יְהִי רָצוֹן מִלְּפָנֶיךָ, יְיָ אֱלֹהֵינוּ וֵאלֹהֵי אֲבוֹתֵינוּ, שֶׁיִּבָּנֶה בֵּית הַמִּקְדָּשׁ בִּמְהֵרָה בְיָמֵינוּ, וְתֵן חֶלְקֵנוּ בְּתוֹרָתֶךָ, וְשָׁם נַעֲבָדְךָ בְּיִרְאָה כִּימֵי עוֹלָם וּכְשָׁנִים קַדְמוֹנִיּוֹת. וְעָרְבָה לַייָ מִנְחַת יְהוּדָה וִירוּשָׁלָיִם, כִּימֵי עוֹלָם וּכְשָׁנִים קַדְמוֹנִיּוֹת.

**Y'hi** ratzon mil-fanecha, Adonoi Elohaynu vay-lohay avotaynu, she-yibaneh bayt ha-mikdash bim'hayra v'yamaynu, v'tayn chelkaynu b'Torah-techa, v'sham na-avadcha b'yira kimay olam u-ch'shanim kadmoniyot. V'arva la-Adonoi minchat Yehuda vi-Yerushalayim ki-may olam u-ch'shanim kadmoniyot.

**May** it be Your will, God, our God, and the God of our ancestors, that You build the Holy Temple quickly and in our days, and give us our place in Your Torah. There,

Daily Prayers

may we worship You in reverence, like in the days of old and in bygone years. And may the offerings of Judah and Jerusalem be favorable before God like in the days of old and in bygone years.

Take three steps forward. This concludes the Amidah service.

# Torah Reading FOR MONDAYS, THURSDAYS, AND SHABBAT

## REMOVING THE TORAH FROM THE ARK

The Torah is the portable symbol of the Jewish people. No matter where we have roamed, or which part of the world you may find yourself, the iconic Torah scroll remains identical. Every letter, every dot, every embellishment, is proscribed in our tradition, and remains the same no matter what.

וַיְהִי בִּנְסֹעַ הָאָרֹן וַיֹּאמֶר מֹשֶׁה, קוּמָה, יְיָ, וְיָפֻצוּ אֹיְבֶיךָ, וְיָנֻסוּ מְשַׂנְאֶיךָ מִפָּנֶיךָ. כִּי מִצִּיּוֹן תֵּצֵא תוֹרָה, וּדְבַר יְיָ מִירוּשָׁלָיִם. בָּרוּךְ שֶׁנָּתַן תּוֹרָה לְעַמּוֹ יִשְׂרָאֵל בִּקְדֻשָּׁתוֹ.

**Va-y'hi** bin-so-ah ha-aron, va-yomer Moshe, kuma Adonoi, v'yafutzu oyvecha, v'yanusu m'sanecha mi-panecha, ki mi-tziyon tay-tzay Torah, u-dvar Adonoi mi-Yerushalayim. Baruch she-natan Torah l'amo Yisrael bik-dushato.

**And** it was, when the Ark would travel, that Moses would say: "Arise, God, and may Your enemies scatter, and may Your haters flee from before You." For Torah *emanates from Zion, and God's word, from Jerusalem. Blessed is He Who has given Torah to His nation Israel, in His holiness.*

God, as I stand here in the synagogue, I understand that all synagogues around the world have features in common. All have a *ner tamid*, an "eternal light." All have Hebrew words and phrases. And all have an Ark to hold our precious Torah scrolls. But back in the day, when we lived in the Land of Israel with Joshua, the Ark held the actual tablets that Moses brought from Heaven! And we traveled through the desert for 40 years with that Ark! We took care of it, we treated it with reverence, and it went everywhere we did. This Ark that I am looking at is reminiscent of that miraculous era.

בֵּהּ אֲנָא רָחִיץ, וְלִשְׁמֵהּ קַדִּישָׁא יַקִּירָא אֲנָא אֵמַר תֻּשְׁבְּחָן. יְהֵא רַעֲוָא קֳדָמָךְ דְּתִפְתַּח לִבַּאי בְּאוֹרַיְתָא, וְתַשְׁלִים מִשְׁאֲלִין דְּלִבַּאי, וְלִבָּא דְכָל עַמָּךְ יִשְׂרָאֵל, לְטַב וּלְחַיִּין וְלִשְׁלָם. (אָמֵן.)

**Bay** *ana rachitz, v'lishmay kadisha yakira, ana aymar, tushbechan. Ye-hay ra-ava kadamach d'tiftach li-ba-ee b'orayta. V'tashlim mishalim di-li-ba-ee, v'liba d'chol amach Yisrael, l'tav u-l'chaim v'lishlam, amen.*

**In** *Him I trust, and to His sacred and holy name I will say praises. May it be Your will that You open my heart to Torah, and that You fulfill the wishes of my heart and the heart of all Your people Israel for goodness, life, and peace. Amen.*

In this moment, I pray, God, that You open my heart to the beauty and wisdom contained in that ancient Ark and in our Ark right here today. Look inside my heart, see my deepest wishes and fulfill them. For good. For life. For peace. Amen.

---

IN THIS MOMENT, I PRAY, GOD, THAT YOU OPEN MY HEART TO THE BEAUTY AND WISDOM CONTAINED IN THAT ANCIENT ARK AND IN OUR ARK RIGHT HERE TODAY.

---

שְׁמַע יִשְׂרָאֵל, יְיָ אֱלֹהֵינוּ, יְיָ אֶחָד.

**Shema** Yisrael, Adonoi Elohaynu, Adonoi Echad.

**Hear,** O Israel, the Lord is our God, the Lord is one.

I reaffirm in this moment that God is one. He is it. He is the only power.

אֶחָד אֱלֹהֵינוּ, גָּדוֹל אֲדוֹנֵנוּ, קָדוֹשׁ שְׁמוֹ.

**Echad** Elohaynu, gadol adonainu, kadosh shmo.

**Our** God is One, our Master is great, His name is holy.

God, You're One, You're great, and You're holy. That's the essence of it all.

### AFTER THE TORAH READING

The Torah is lifted for all to see.

וְזֹאת הַתּוֹרָה אֲשֶׁר שָׂם מֹשֶׁה לִפְנֵי בְּנֵי יִשְׂרָאֵל, עַל פִּי יְיָ בְּיַד מֹשֶׁה.

**V'zot** ha-Torah asher sam Moshe lifnay bnai Yisrael al pi Adonoi b'yad Moshe.

God, we affirm right here that this is the very same Torah that You gave to Moses thousands of years ago.

עֵץ חַיִּים הִיא לַמַּחֲזִיקִים בָּהּ, וְתֹמְכֶיהָ מְאֻשָּׁר. דְּרָכֶיהָ דַרְכֵי נֹעַם, וְכָל נְתִיבוֹתֶיהָ שָׁלוֹם. אֹרֶךְ יָמִים בִּימִינָהּ, בִּשְׂמֹאלָהּ עֹשֶׁר וְכָבוֹד. יְיָ חָפֵץ לְמַעַן צִדְקוֹ, יַגְדִּיל תּוֹרָה וְיַאְדִּיר.

**Etz** *chaim hee la-machazikim bah, v'tomche-ha me-ushar, dera-chehah darchay noam, v'chol netivoteha shalom. Orech yamim bi-minah, bi-smolah osher v'kavod, Adonoi chafetz l'ma-an tzidko, yagdil Torah v'yadir.*

**The** *Torah is a tree of life for those who grasp it, and its supporters are fortunate. Its ways are ways of pleasantness, and all its paths are peace. Long life is at its right; at its left is wealth and honor. God desired for the sake of His righteousness — may Torah be magnified and strengthened.*

The Torah is life. In it are deep, contemporary truths for living, for parenting, for relationships, for morality. I want to hang onto that, God, like a dying person clings to life. Everything about Torah is beautiful, and it's our job to make sure our observance of it is beautiful, and that, as the Chosen People, we are kind and pleasant, since we represent it. It's a responsibility which we are proud and privileged to accept.

# Kaddish

The Kaddish prayer is a central piece of Jewish spirituality. There are a few different versions of the Kaddish. It is sometimes used as a closing to one section of the prayers. It is famously recited by mourners to pay tribute to God and to their loved ones that have passed.

Daily Prayers

Yet, most Jews do not know what the words of Kaddish mean. Saying "amen" and other responses, where indicated in bolded brackets below, to someone else's Kaddish, is considered a momentous opportunity to show respect and honor to God and to the deceased.

יִתְגַּדַּל וְיִתְקַדַּשׁ שְׁמֵהּ רַבָּא. בְּעָלְמָא דִּי בְרָא כִרְעוּתֵהּ, וְיַמְלִיךְ מַלְכוּתֵהּ בְּחַיֵּיכוֹן וּבְיוֹמֵיכוֹן וּבְחַיֵּי דְכָל בֵּית יִשְׂרָאֵל, בַּעֲגָלָא וּבִזְמַן קָרִיב, וְאִמְרוּ אָמֵן.

יְהֵא שְׁמֵהּ רַבָּא מְבָרַךְ לְעָלַם וּלְעָלְמֵי עָלְמַיָּא.

יִתְבָּרַךְ וְיִשְׁתַּבַּח וְיִתְפָּאַר וְיִתְרוֹמַם וְיִתְנַשֵּׂא וְיִתְהַדָּר וְיִתְעַלֶּה וְיִתְהַלָּל שְׁמֵהּ דְּקֻדְשָׁא בְּרִיךְ הוּא, לְעֵלָּא מִן כָּל [בעשי״ת לְעֵלָּא וּלְעֵלָּא מִכָּל] בִּרְכָתָא וְשִׁירָתָא תֻּשְׁבְּחָתָא וְנֶחֱמָתָא, דַּאֲמִירָן בְּעָלְמָא, וְאִמְרוּ אָמֵן.

תִּתְקַבֵּל צְלוֹתְהוֹן וּבָעוּתְהוֹן דְּכָל (בֵּית) יִשְׂרָאֵל קֳדָם אֲבוּהוֹן דִּי בִשְׁמַיָּא וְאִמְרוּ אָמֵן.

יְהֵא שְׁלָמָא רַבָּא מִן שְׁמַיָּא, וְחַיִּים (טוֹבִים) עָלֵינוּ וְעַל כָּל יִשְׂרָאֵל, וְאִמְרוּ אָמֵן.

עֹשֶׂה שָׁלוֹם [בעשי״ת יש אומרים: הַשָּׁלוֹם] בִּמְרוֹמָיו, הוּא יַעֲשֶׂה שָׁלוֹם עָלֵינוּ וְעַל כָּל יִשְׂרָאֵל, וְאִמְרוּ אָמֵן.

**Yit-gadal** *v'yit-kadash shemay rabbah* **[Amen]**. *B'alma di vra chirutay v'yamlich malchutay b'cha-yaychon u-v'yomaychon u-v'cha-yay d'chol bait Yisrael, ba-agalah u-vi-zman kariv v'imru amen* **[Amen, yehay shmay rabbah m'varach l'alam u-l'olmay ul-mayah]**. *Yit-barach v'yish-tabach v'yit-pa-ar v'yit-romam v'yit-nasay, v'yit-hadar v'yit-aleh v'yit-hallal, shmay d'kudsha brich hu* **[Brich hu]**. *L'ayla min kol birchata v'shirata,* *tush-b'chata, v'nechamata, da-amiran b'alma, v'imru amen* **[Amen]**. *Yehay shlama rabbah min shamaya, v'chaim alaynu v'al kol Yisrael, v'imru amen* **[Amen]**.

**Oseh** *shalom bi-mromav, hu ya-aseh shalom alaynu, v'al kol Yisrael, v'imru amen* **[Amen]**.

**May** *His great name be magnified and sanctified* **[Amen]** *in the world that He created, and may His kingdom reign, in our lifetimes, and in our days, and in the lives of all the house of Israel, speedily, and in an imminent time, and may we say amen* **[Amen, yehay shmay rabbah m'varach l'alam u-l'olmay ul-mayah]**. *May His holy name be blessed, praised, glorified, exalted, raised up, honored, elevated, lauded — blessed is He* **[Blessed is He]** *— above all blessings, songs, praises, and comforting words, that are spoken in the world, and may we say amen* **[Amen]**. *May there be much peace from heaven, and life, upon us and on all of Israel, and may we say amen* **[Amen]**. *He Who creates peace in the heavens, may He create peace on us, and on all of Israel, and may we say amen* **[Amen]**.

---

You are great, God. Even though You take people in old age — and sometimes in their prime. Either way, it hurts to lose someone you love. And sometimes, if those relationships were complicated, it hurts even more, because there are no more tomorrows in which to fix it.

But, God, in Judaism we affirm that You are good. No, great. And that's what I want to say in Kaddish, God, when I think of loss — that with all those that have lived and died, You, God remain. And although I may never understand Your ways, I wish to affirm my belief that You are good, and always will be good.

So therefore, I ask You, God: please send lots of blessings to all the good people in this world, and to those who study Your Torah and teach it. Send them life, peace, joy, health, livelihood, and mercy. And please help those who perhaps aren't so good to become better people.

May He Who makes peace in the heavens, also make peace on all of us, and on all of Israel. Amen.

# *Alaynu*

Alaynu is the closing of each prayer service — or, for most of us, the signal that Kiddush is coming soon! Its rousing energy bespeaks its powerful themes — of Jews being different; of a wish for utopia; of repairing the world under the banner of ethical monotheism.

עָלֵינוּ לְשַׁבֵּחַ לַאֲדוֹן הַכֹּל, לָתֵת גְּדֻלָּה לְיוֹצֵר בְּרֵאשִׁית, שֶׁלֹּא עָשָׂנוּ כְּגוֹיֵי הָאֲרָצוֹת, וְלֹא שָׂמָנוּ כְּמִשְׁפְּחוֹת הָאֲדָמָה, שֶׁלֹּא שָׂם חֶלְקֵנוּ כָּהֶם, וְגוֹרָלֵנוּ כְּכָל הֲמוֹנָם, וַאֲנַחְנוּ כּוֹרְעִים וּמִשְׁתַּחֲוִים וּמוֹדִים, לִפְנֵי מֶלֶךְ מַלְכֵי הַמְּלָכִים, הַקָּדוֹשׁ בָּרוּךְ הוּא. שֶׁהוּא נוֹטֶה שָׁמַיִם וְיֹסֵד אָרֶץ, וּמוֹשַׁב יְקָרוֹ בַּשָּׁמַיִם מִמַּעַל, וּשְׁכִינַת עֻזּוֹ בְּגָבְהֵי מְרוֹמִים, הוּא אֱלֹהֵינוּ אֵין עוֹד. אֱמֶת מַלְכֵּנוּ, אֶפֶס זוּלָתוֹ, כַּכָּתוּב בְּתוֹרָתוֹ: וְיָדַעְתָּ הַיּוֹם וַהֲשֵׁבֹתָ אֶל לְבָבֶךָ, כִּי יְיָ הוּא הָאֱלֹהִים בַּשָּׁמַיִם מִמַּעַל, וְעַל הָאָרֶץ מִתָּחַת, אֵין עוֹד.

עַל כֵּן נְקַוֶּה לְךָ יְיָ אֱלֹהֵינוּ, לִרְאוֹת מְהֵרָה בְּתִפְאֶרֶת עֻזֶּךָ, לְהַעֲבִיר גִּלּוּלִים מִן הָאָרֶץ, וְהָאֱלִילִים כָּרוֹת יִכָּרֵתוּן, לְתַקֵּן עוֹלָם בְּמַלְכוּת שַׁדַּי, וְכָל בְּנֵי בָשָׂר יִקְרְאוּ בִשְׁמֶךָ, לְהַפְנוֹת אֵלֶיךָ כָּל רִשְׁעֵי אָרֶץ. יַכִּירוּ וְיֵדְעוּ כָּל יוֹשְׁבֵי תֵבֵל, כִּי לְךָ

תִּכְרַע כָּל בֶּרֶךְ, תִּשָּׁבַע כָּל לָשׁוֹן. לְפָנֶיךָ יְיָ אֱלֹהֵינוּ יִכְרְעוּ וְיִפֹּלוּ, וְלִכְבוֹד שִׁמְךָ יְקָר יִתֵּנוּ, וִיקַבְּלוּ כֻלָּם אֶת עֹל מַלְכוּתֶךָ, וְתִמְלֹךְ עֲלֵיהֶם מְהֵרָה לְעוֹלָם וָעֶד. כִּי הַמַּלְכוּת שֶׁלְּךָ הִיא, וּלְעוֹלְמֵי עַד תִּמְלוֹךְ בְּכָבוֹד, כַּכָּתוּב בְּתוֹרָתֶךָ, יְיָ יִמְלֹךְ לְעוֹלָם וָעֶד. וְנֶאֱמַר, וְהָיָה יְיָ לְמֶלֶךְ עַל כָּל הָאָרֶץ, בַּיּוֹם הַהוּא יִהְיֶה יְיָ אֶחָד, וּשְׁמוֹ אֶחָד.

**Alaynu** l'shabayach la-adon ha-kol, la-tet gedulah l'yotzer braysheet. Shelo asanu l'goyay ha-aratzot, v'lo samanu k'mishpachot ha-adama. Shelo sam chelkaynu ka-hem, v'goralaynu k'chol hamonam. Va-anachnu korim, u-mish-tachavim u-modim, lifnay melech malchay ha-melachim, ha-Kadosh Baruch Hu. Shehu noteh shamayim v'yosed aretz, u-moshav yekaro ba-shamayim mi-ma-al, u-shechinat uzo b'gav-hay m'romim. Hu Elohaynu ayn od, emet malkaynu efes zulato. Ka-katuv b'torato, v'yadata hayom v'hashay-vota el levavecha, ki Adonoi hu ha-elohim, ba-shamayim mi-ma-al, v'al ha-aretz mi-tachat ayn od.

**Al** kayn nekaveh l'cha Adonoi Elohaynu, lirot m'hayra b'tiferet uzecha. L'ha-avir gilulim min ha-aretz, v'ha-elilim karot yi-karaytun. L'taken olam b'malchut Shaday, v'chol bnai vasar yikr'u vi-shmecha, l'hafnot ay-lecha kol rishay aretz, yakiru v'yay-du kol yoshvay tayvel, ki l'cha tichra kol berech, ti-shava kol lashon. L'fanecha Adonoi Elohaynu yichr'u v'yipolu, v'lichvod shimcha yekar yitaynu. Vi-kablu kulam et ol malchutecha, v'timloch alayhem m'hayra l'olam va-ed, ki ha-malchut shelcha hee, u-l'olmay ad, timloch b'chavod. Kakatuv b'Torah-techa, Adonoi yimloch l'olam va-ed. V'ne-emar, v'haya

*Adonoi l'melech al kol ha-aretz, ba-yom ha-hu y'hiyeh Adonoi echad, u-sh'mo echad.*

**It** is incumbent on us to praise the Master of all, to give grandeur to He Who fashioned creation. For He didn't make us like all the nations of the world, nor did He make us like the families of the world. He didn't make our lot like theirs; nor our portion like all their multitudes. We bend, bow and give thanks before the King of all kings, the Holy one, blessed is He. For He bends heavens and establishes earth, and His treasured seat is in the heavens above, and the strength of His presence is in the highest heights. He is our God; there is none other. Our King is true; there is nothingness besides Him. As it is written in His Torah, "And may you know today, and bring it close to your heart, that God is the Lord in the heavens above and on the earth below" — there is none other.

**And** therefore we hope to You, God, our God, to quickly see the glory of Your might; to remove idolatry from the earth and to cut off false gods; to repair the world in the kingship of God, and that all humans call in Your name. May all the wicked of the earth turn to You, and may all the world's citizens recognize and know You. May all knees bend to You, and all tongues swear to You. May they all bow and fall before You, God, our God, and may they give value to the honor of Your name. May they all accept the yoke of Your kingship, and may You reign over them quickly and forever, for kingship is Yours, and You will rule in honor forever and ever. As it says in Your Torah, "God will reign forever and ever!"

*And it is said, "God will be King over all the earth. On that day, God will be One and His name will be One."*

God, it is our job, and I'm not saying we're always very good at it, to constantly remember how lucky we are to be Jewish. I am so grateful to have You, the Jewish God. And while I physically bow my body toward You, I remind myself to inwardly submit to You and to remember that You run the show. You, literally, are the ultimate power with no comparison. It's an effort to constantly remember this, but that's why I'm here, right?

Therefore, I'm hoping, God, for a time when the whole world can understand this truth, and can help fix the world under Your watch and within Your vision. I'm praying for that time when evil will vanish, because everyone recognizes Who You are. I pray that it remain this way for always, and that Your Oneness and perfection will bring in world peace once and for all.

# Nighttime Shema

*The Shema is recited at night before one goes to sleep, as a declaration of faith and trust during a time when people are likely to feel scared and vulnerable. Often as one goes to bed, all his fears and ruminations emerge and seem scarier and more difficult than during the day. In the collection of prayers of the nighttime Shema, we turn our worries over to God and trust him with our souls while we sleep. Below appear some of the highlights of the nighttime Shema.*

**שְׁמַע** | יִשְׂרָאֵל, יְיָ | אֱלֹהֵינוּ, יְיָ | אֶחָד.

**בָּרוּךְ** שֵׁם כְּבוֹד מַלְכוּתוֹ לְעוֹלָם וָעֶד.

**Daily Prayers**    89

**Shema** *Yisrael, Adonoi Elohaynu, Adonoi echad.*

**Baruch** *shem k'vod malchuto l'olam va-ed.*

**Hear,** O Israel, God is our God; God is One.

**Blessed** is the name of the honor of His kingdom for all eternity.

וְאָהַבְתָּ אֵת יְיָ ׀ אֱלֹהֶיךָ, בְּכָל ׀ לְבָבְךָ, וּבְכָל נַפְשְׁךָ, וּבְכָל מְאֹדֶךָ. וְהָיוּ הַדְּבָרִים הָאֵלֶּה, אֲשֶׁר ׀ אָנֹכִי מְצַוְּךָ הַיּוֹם, עַל ׀ לְבָבֶךָ. וְשִׁנַּנְתָּם לְבָנֶיךָ, וְדִבַּרְתָּ בָּם, בְּשִׁבְתְּךָ בְּבֵיתֶךָ, וּבְלֶכְתְּךָ בַדֶּרֶךְ, וּבְשָׁכְבְּךָ, וּבְקוּמֶךָ. וּקְשַׁרְתָּם לְאוֹת ׀ עַל יָדֶךָ, וְהָיוּ לְטֹטָפֹת בֵּין ׀ עֵינֶיךָ. וּכְתַבְתָּם ׀ עַל מְזֻזוֹת בֵּיתֶךָ וּבִשְׁעָרֶיךָ.

**V'ahavta** *ayt Adonoi Elohecha, b'chol l'vav'cha, u-v'chol naf-sh'cha, u-v'chol m'odecha. V'hayu ha-d'varim ha-ayleh, asher anochi m'tzav-cha ha-yom, al l'vavecha. V'shi-nantam l'vanecha v'dibarta bam, b'shiv-t'cha b'vay-techa u-v'lech-t'cha va-derech, u-v'shach-b'cha u-v'kumecha. U-k'shartam l'ot al yadecha, v'hayu l'totafot bayn aynecha. U-ch'tavtam al mezuzot baytecha u-visharecha.*

**You** shall love God, your God with all your heart and with all your soul and with all your might. May these words that I am commanding you today be on your heart. Teach them to your children and speak of them when you sit in your home and when you travel on the road; when you lie down and when you arise. Tie them as a sign on your arm and may they be phylacteries between your eyes. And write them on mezuzah scrolls on the doorposts of your homes and gates.

God, the concept of loving You can be hard — how does one love a "Being" that cannot be grasped with the five senses? But I am going to try, God — with all my heart, soul, and energy. I would like to become more connected to this idea, not just at synagogue, but at home. Not just for me, but to speak of it openly with my children. Not just on special occasions, but daily. And God, when I see the mezuzah on my door, whose scroll contains these concepts, I will remember that my home is an oasis of spirituality and God-awareness in a sad and sometimes empty and confusing world.

Thank You, God, for the gift of loving You.

הַשְׁכִּיבֵנוּ יְיָ אֱלֹהֵינוּ לְשָׁלוֹם, וְהַעֲמִידֵנוּ מַלְכֵּנוּ לְחַיִּים, וּפְרוֹשׂ עָלֵינוּ סֻכַּת שְׁלוֹמֶךָ, וְתַקְּנֵנוּ בְּעֵצָה טוֹבָה מִלְּפָנֶיךָ, וְהוֹשִׁיעֵנוּ לְמַעַן שְׁמֶךָ. וְהָגֵן בַּעֲדֵנוּ, וְהָסֵר מֵעָלֵינוּ אוֹיֵב, דֶּבֶר, וְחֶרֶב, וְרָעָב, וְיָגוֹן, וְהָסֵר שָׂטָן מִלְּפָנֵינוּ וּמֵאַחֲרֵינוּ, וּבְצֵל כְּנָפֶיךָ תַּסְתִּירֵנוּ, כִּי אֵל שׁוֹמְרֵנוּ וּמַצִּילֵנוּ אָתָּה, כִּי אֵל מֶלֶךְ חַנּוּן וְרַחוּם אָתָּה, וּשְׁמוֹר צֵאתֵנוּ וּבוֹאֵנוּ, לְחַיִּים וּלְשָׁלוֹם, מֵעַתָּה וְעַד עוֹלָם.

***Hashkivay-nu*** Adonoi Elohaynu l'shalom, v'ha-amiday-nu malkaynu l'chaim, u-frose alaynu sukkat shlomecha, v'taknaynu b'eitzah tova mil-fanecha, v'ho-shi-aynu l'ma-an sh'mecha. V'hagen ba-adaynu v'haser may-alaynu oyev, dever, v'cherev, v'ra-av, v'yagon, v'haser satan mil-fanaynu u-may-acharaynu, u-v'tzel k'nafecha tastiraynu, ki El shom-raynu u-ma-tzilaynu Ata, ki El melech chanun v'rachum Ata, u-shmor tzay-taynu u-vo-aynu, l'chaim u-l'shalom, may-ata v'ad olam.

**Lay** *us down, God, our God, in peace, and stand us back up, our King, for life, and spread over us the shelter of Your peace, and establish for us good advice before You, and save us, for Your name's sake. And be a shield on our behalf, and remove from before us enemies, plagues, sword, hunger, and agony; and remove Satan from before us and from behind us, and conceal us in the shade of Your wings; for You are a God Who guards and saves us; for You are a God and King Who is compassionate and merciful. Guard our goings and comings in life and peace, from now and until forever.*

God, as I lay down to sleep I can't help but ruminate about all my doings today. Please let my sleep be in peace and allow me to wake up tomorrow morning healthy, whole, and peaceful. Let my worries seem smaller tomorrow; let my night's sleep bring good counsel and better ideas. Things always seem better in the morning, God, so please make this be so! Help me to sleep peacefully, free of worry, rumination, guilt, and what-ifs. Don't let my night be punctuated by negative thoughts or fears. Let me feel confident for the future and peaceful and serene about the past. I want to feel Your reassuring presence wherever I go.

---

LET MY WORRIES SEEM SMALLER TOMORROW; LET MY NIGHT'S SLEEP BRING GOOD COUNSEL AND BETTER IDEAS.

---

*The following paragraph is the prayer that our patriarch Jacob uttered upon first meeting his grandchildren when he was reunited with his son Joseph after so many years. This sincere, brief, and heartfelt prayer — that the next generation be blessed with angelic protection and enjoy the future of home and family — is one that transcends the ages. May we, too, as the descendants of Jacob, be blessed with these things.*

**הַמַּלְאָךְ** הַגֹּאֵל אֹתִי מִכָּל רָע יְבָרֵךְ אֶת הַנְּעָרִים, וְיִקָּרֵא בָהֶם שְׁמִי וְשֵׁם אֲבוֹתַי אַבְרָהָם וְיִצְחָק, וְיִדְגּוּ לָרֹב בְּקֶרֶב הָאָרֶץ.

**Hamalach** ha-go-el oti mi-kol rah, y'varech et ha-n'arim v'yi-karay vahem sh'mi v'shem avotai Avraham v'Yitzchak, v'yid-gu larov b'kerev ha-aretz.

**The** angel who redeemed me from all evil will bless the young boys, and may my name, and the names of my fathers Abraham and Isaac, be called upon them, and may they multiply like fish in the midst of the land.

These verses are recited three times each.

**יְבָרֶכְךָ** יְיָ וְיִשְׁמְרֶךָ. יָאֵר יְיָ פָּנָיו אֵלֶיךָ וִיחֻנֶּךָּ. יִשָּׂא יְיָ פָּנָיו אֵלֶיךָ וְיָשֵׂם לְךָ שָׁלוֹם.

**Y'varech'cha** Adonoi v'yish-m'recha. Ya-er Adonoi panav ay-lecha vi-chuneka. Yisa Adonoi panav ay-lecha v'yasem l'cha shalom.

**May** God bless you and watch over you. May God shine His face toward you and favor you. May God lift His face toward you and give you peace.

**הִנֵּה** לֹא יָנוּם וְלֹא יִישָׁן שׁוֹמֵר יִשְׂרָאֵל.

**Hi-nay** lo yanum v'lo yishan shomer Yisrael.

**Behold,** the Guardian of Israel neither slumbers nor sleeps.

לִישׁוּעָתְךָ קִוִּיתִי יְיָ. קִוִּיתִי לִישׁוּעָתְךָ יְיָ. יְיָ לִישׁוּעָתְךָ קִוִּיתִי.

**Li-shu-atcha** kiviti Adonoi. Kiviti Adonoi li-shu-atcha. Adonoi li-shu-atcha kiviti.

**For** Your salvation I have hoped, God. I have hoped, God, for Your salvation. God, for Your salvation, I have hoped.

בְּשֵׁם יְיָ אֱלֹהֵי יִשְׂרָאֵל, מִימִינִי מִיכָאֵל, וּמִשְּׂמֹאלִי גַּבְרִיאֵל, וּמִלְּפָנַי אוּרִיאֵל, וּמֵאֲחוֹרַי רְפָאֵל, וְעַל רֹאשִׁי שְׁכִינַת אֵל.

**B'shem** Adonoi Elohay Yisrael, mi-mini Michael, u-mi-smo-li Gavriel, u-mil-fanai Uriel, u-may-acharai Rephael. V'al roshi shechinat El.

**In** the name of God, the God of Israel: at my right is the angel Michael; at my left is the angel Gabriel; before me is the angel Uriel; behind me is the angel Raphael. And upon my head is the divine presence of God.

*Many conclude the nighttime Shema with the recitation of "Adon Olam" (below) and the prayer for "Forgiveness" on page 185.*

# Adon Olam

Adon Olam is both the closing prayer of the nighttime Shema and a poetic prayer in its own right — often used to begin or close the service at synagogue. It is one of the most famous parts of Jewish prayer, as popularized in Jewish camps everywhere. Its meter is *suited for almost any sixteen-beat tune, so it's been set to all kinds of melodies, from Jewish to pop culture. Yet, for all its campy spunk, Adon Olam is a deeply meaningful, reassuring, and kabbalistically-inspired poetic offering about the very essence of God Himself.*

---

YET, FOR ALL ITS CAMPY SPUNK, ADON OLAM IS A DEEPLY MEANINGFUL, REASSURING, AND KABBALISTICALLY-INSPIRED POETIC OFFERING ABOUT THE VERY ESSENCE OF GOD HIMSELF.

---

אֲדוֹן עוֹלָם אֲשֶׁר מָלַךְ, בְּטֶרֶם כָּל יְצִיר נִבְרָא. לְעֵת נַעֲשָׂה בְחֶפְצוֹ כֹּל, אֲזַי מֶלֶךְ שְׁמוֹ נִקְרָא. וְאַחֲרֵי כִּכְלוֹת הַכֹּל, לְבַדּוֹ יִמְלוֹךְ נוֹרָא. וְהוּא הָיָה, וְהוּא הֹוֶה, וְהוּא יִהְיֶה, בְּתִפְאָרָה. וְהוּא אֶחָד וְאֵין שֵׁנִי, לְהַמְשִׁיל לוֹ לְהַחְבִּירָה. בְּלִי רֵאשִׁית בְּלִי תַכְלִית, וְלוֹ הָעֹז וְהַמִּשְׂרָה. וְהוּא אֵלִי וְחַי גֹּאֲלִי, וְצוּר חֶבְלִי בְּעֵת צָרָה. וְהוּא נִסִּי וּמָנוֹס לִי, מְנָת כּוֹסִי בְּיוֹם אֶקְרָא. בְּיָדוֹ אַפְקִיד רוּחִי, בְּעֵת אִישַׁן וְאָעִירָה. וְעִם רוּחִי גְוִיָּתִי, יְיָ לִי וְלֹא אִירָא.

**Adon** olam asher malach, b'terem kol y'tzir nivra

l'ayt naso b'cheftzo kol, azai melech sh'mo nikra

V'acharay kichlot ha-kol, le-vado yimloch nora

v'hu haya, v'hu hoveh, v'hu y'hiyeh b'tifarah.

V'hu echad, v'ayn shayni, l'hamshilo l'hachbirah

b'li raysheet, b'li tachlit, v'lo ha-oz v'hamisra

V'hu ay-li, v'chai go-ali, v'tzur chevli b'ayt tzarah,

v'hu nisi u-manos li, m'nat kosi b'yom ekra

B'yado afkid ruchi, b'ayt ishan v'a-ira,

v'im ruchi g'viyati, Adonoi li v'lo irah.

Daily Prayers 95

**Master** *of the world, Who ruled before any being was created: at the time that there arose in His will [to create] everything, he was then called "King."*

*And after everything has ceased to be, He alone will rule awesomely. He was, He is, and He will always exist in splendor.*

*And He is One, and there is no other that can compare to Him or be an equal; with no beginning and no end, and rulership and strength are His alone.*

*And He is my God and my living redeemer, the Rock in my pain at times of distress; and He is my banner and refuge for me, the portion in my cup on the day I call.*

*In His hand I entrust my spirit when I go to bed — and I will awaken! With my spirit is also my body — God is mine, and I shall not fear.*

God, it's so hard for our finite minds to conceptualize this, but we affirm in this song that You existed before anything else was here in this world. Before all life — plants, trees, mountains — You were here. But it was only when life came into being, that You became a "king" because then the world could acknowledge Your presence. The same way my mind can't grasp that the numbers are infinite, I can't really grasp that You are infinite. I sing Adon Olam, which teaches all this, because I know it's a central theme in Judaism and this is one of the basics — that You transcend time and space.

The extension of this, God, is that when everything is gone, when this world stops turning and none of us are here... You, God, will still be here! You are One, with no one to compare. Any analogy that even attempts to shed light on Your essence will be inherently flawed, because absolutely no analogy can do justice. Yet, in all that abstract grandeur, You are our

God, and You are our Rock. You care about us deeply and are never too remote to tune into our complicated and even petty needs.

For that reason, God, I feel that I can entrust myself to You, when I wake up and when I go to bed at night. And that is why, God, I know that I need not fear, since Your spirit, Your spark, is always with me.

*Part Two:*

# GRATITUDE AFTER EATING

## [BIRKAT HA-MAZON]

*The "Birkat" — or "bentching" as it's colloquially called ("bentch" means "bless" in Yiddish) — is a song that many know, at least in part. What most people don't know, or at least don't focus on, is what it means. This song is the ultimate gratitude machine. It empowers us to mindfully realize that all our food is a gift, that Israel and Jerusalem are a gift, that being able to feed others is a gift. Our tradition teaches us that the best spiritual trick to earning a good living is to break bread, and afterward, say this prayer with depth and feeling — that remembering where all our gifts come from is the best merit to maintain and earn them.*

---

THIS SONG IS THE ULTIMATE GRATITUDE MACHINE. IT EMPOWERS US TO MINDFULLY REALIZE THAT ALL OUR FOOD IS A GIFT, THAT ISRAEL AND JERUSALEM ARE A GIFT, THAT BEING ABLE TO FEED OTHERS IS A GIFT.

---

## GRATITUDE FOR THE FOOD

בָּרוּךְ אַתָּה יְיָ, אֱלֹהֵינוּ מֶלֶךְ הָעוֹלָם, הַזָּן אֶת הָעוֹלָם כֻּלּוֹ בְּטוּבוֹ בְּחֵן בְּחֶסֶד וּבְרַחֲמִים, הוּא נוֹתֵן לֶחֶם לְכָל בָּשָׂר כִּי לְעוֹלָם חַסְדּוֹ. וּבְטוּבוֹ הַגָּדוֹל תָּמִיד לֹא חָסַר לָנוּ, וְאַל יֶחְסַר לָנוּ מָזוֹן לְעוֹלָם וָעֶד. בַּעֲבוּר שְׁמוֹ הַגָּדוֹל, כִּי הוּא אֵל זָן וּמְפַרְנֵס לַכֹּל וּמֵטִיב לַכֹּל, וּמֵכִין מָזוֹן לְכָל בְּרִיּוֹתָיו אֲשֶׁר בָּרָא. בָּרוּךְ אַתָּה יְיָ, הַזָּן אֶת הַכֹּל.

**Baruch** Ata Adonoi, Elohaynu melech ha-olam, hazan et ha-olam kulo b'tuvo, b'chayn b'chesed u-v'rachamim. Hu notayn lechem l'chol basar, ki l'olam chasdo. U-v'tuvo ha-gadol, tamid lo cha-sar lanu, v'al yech-sar lanu, mazon l'olam va-ed. Ba-avur shemo ha-gadol, ki hu El zan u-m'farnes la-kol, u-maytiv la-kol u-maychin mazon l'chol bri-otav asher bara. Baruch Ata Adonoi, ha-zan et ha-kol.

*Gratitude After Eating*

***Blessed*** *are You, God, our God, King of the universe, Who sustains the entire world with His goodness, with grace, with kindness, and with compassion. He gives bread to all flesh, for His kindness endures forever. And in His great goodness, He has never caused us to lack, nor ever will cause us to lack sustenance, forever. For the sake of His great name, for He is the God Who feeds and sustains all, and is good to all, and prepares food for all His creatures that He created. Blessed are You, God, Who feeds all.*

Dear God, I want to take a moment — or a few — to acknowledge my gratitude for the daily sustenance that You provide. With kindness and generosity, You nourish the whole world with enough food. You allow us to share, in some small way, in making sure everyone gets what they need, by commanding us to share of our bounty with those who are needier than we are. You provide delicious, fresh, healthy, beautiful food that You make available so easily to me. You create food that is good-tasting, good for my body, good for my soul, and colorful to look at. I have never been so needy that I've had to go hungry, and for this I am so grateful.

## GRATITUDE FOR ISRAEL

נוֹדֶה לְךָ, יְיָ אֱלֹהֵינוּ, עַל שֶׁהִנְחַלְתָּ לַאֲבוֹתֵינוּ אֶרֶץ חֶמְדָּה טוֹבָה וּרְחָבָה, וְעַל שֶׁהוֹצֵאתָנוּ, יְיָ אֱלֹהֵינוּ, מֵאֶרֶץ מִצְרַיִם, וּפְדִיתָנוּ מִבֵּית עֲבָדִים, וְעַל בְּרִיתְךָ שֶׁחָתַמְתָּ בִּבְשָׂרֵנוּ, וְעַל תּוֹרָתְךָ שֶׁלִּמַּדְתָּנוּ, וְעַל חֻקֶּיךָ שֶׁהוֹדַעְתָּנוּ, וְעַל חַיִּים חֵן וָחֶסֶד שֶׁחוֹנַנְתָּנוּ, וְעַל אֲכִילַת מָזוֹן שָׁאַתָּה זָן וּמְפַרְנֵס אוֹתָנוּ תָּמִיד, בְּכָל יוֹם וּבְכָל עֵת וּבְכָל שָׁעָה.

וְעַל הַכֹּל, יְיָ אֱלֹהֵינוּ, אֲנַחְנוּ מוֹדִים לָךְ, וּמְבָרְכִים אוֹתָךְ, יִתְבָּרַךְ שִׁמְךָ בְּפִי כָּל חַי תָּמִיד לְעוֹלָם וָעֶד. כַּכָּתוּב, וְאָכַלְתָּ וְשָׂבָעְתָּ, וּבֵרַכְתָּ אֶת יְיָ אֱלֹהֶיךָ עַל הָאָרֶץ הַטֹּבָה אֲשֶׁר נָתַן לָךְ. בָּרוּךְ אַתָּה יְיָ, עַל הָאָרֶץ וְעַל הַמָּזוֹן.

**Nodeh** l'cha Adonoi Elohaynu al she-hin-chalta la-avotay-nu eretz chemda tova u-r'chava, v'al she-hotzay-tanu Adonoi Elohaynu may-eretz mitzrayim, uf-di-tanu mi-bayt avadim, v'al brit-cha she-cha-tamta biv-saraynu, v'al torat-cha she-limad'tanu, v'al chu-kecha she-ho-datanu, v'al chaim chayn va-chesed she-cho-nantanu, v'al achilat mazon she-Ata zan, u-m'farnes otanu tamid b'chol yom, u-v'chol ayt u-v'chol sha-ah.

**V'al** ha-kol Adonoi Elohaynu anachnu modim lach u-mevarchim otach, yit-barach shimcha b'fi kol chai tamid l'olam va-ed. Kakatuv, v'achalta v'savata u-vay-rachta et Adonoi Elohecha al ha-aretz ha-tova asher natan lach. Baruch Ata Adonoi, al ha-aretz v'al ha-mazon.

**We** thank You, God, our God, that You've bequeathed to our ancestors a special, wonderful, spacious land, and that You took us out, God, our God, from the land of Egypt, and redeemed us from the house of slavery, and for the covenant that You stamped into our bodies [bris], and for the Torah that You've taught us, and for the laws that You made known to us, and for the life, grace, and kindness that You've graced us with, and for the eating of the food that You nourish us with, and sustain us with, always — every day, and every hour, and every moment.

Gratitude After Eating

***And*** *for all that, God, our God, we thank You and bless You, may Your name be blessed in the mouths of all living beings always and forever, as it's written: "You shall eat, and you shall be satisfied, and you shall bless the Lord your God, for the good land that He gave you." Blessed are You, God, for the land, and for the food.*

I was hungry, and now I'm full. I recognize that You've commanded us to thank You after we've eaten — not just for the food, but for so many other things. You have done so much for us, personally and historically. When I reflect back on our nation's history, I recognize Your goodness in taking us out of Egypt so that we could be Jewish; giving us the incredible gift of Torah, that we might learn how to be a moral and spiritual people; and giving us the beautiful, fertile land of Israel, of mountains and valleys — and holiness. For all these and so much more, please help me to always remember to thank You. Now, while my stomach is full of delicious food, is the perfect time to be grateful. God, thank You, for being so good to me personally — and to my people — always.

## REMEMBERING JERUSALEM

רַחֵם נָא, יְיָ אֱלֹהֵינוּ, עַל יִשְׂרָאֵל עַמֶּךָ, וְעַל יְרוּשָׁלַיִם עִירֶךָ, וְעַל צִיּוֹן מִשְׁכַּן כְּבוֹדֶךָ, וְעַל מַלְכוּת בֵּית דָּוִד מְשִׁיחֶךָ, וְעַל הַבַּיִת הַגָּדוֹל וְהַקָּדוֹשׁ שֶׁנִּקְרָא שִׁמְךָ עָלָיו. אֱלֹהֵינוּ, אָבִינוּ, רְעֵנוּ, זוּנֵנוּ, פַּרְנְסֵנוּ, וְכַלְכְּלֵנוּ, וְהַרְוִיחֵנוּ, וְהַרְוַח לָנוּ יְיָ אֱלֹהֵינוּ מְהֵרָה מִכָּל צָרוֹתֵינוּ, וְנָא אַל תַּצְרִיכֵנוּ, יְיָ אֱלֹהֵינוּ, לֹא לִידֵי מַתְּנַת בָּשָׂר וָדָם, וְלֹא לִידֵי הַלְוָאָתָם, כִּי אִם לְיָדְךָ הַמְּלֵאָה, הַפְּתוּחָה, הַקְּדוֹשָׁה וְהָרְחָבָה, שֶׁלֹא נֵבוֹשׁ וְלֹא נִכָּלֵם לְעוֹלָם וָעֶד.

***Rachem*** *na, Adonoi Elohaynu, al Yisrael amecha v'al Yerushalayim irecha, v'al tziyon mishkan k'vodecha, v'al malchut bayt David m'shi-checha, v'al ha-bayit ha-gadol v'ha-kadosh she-nikra shimcha alav. Elohaynu, avinu, r'aynu, zu-naynu, parnesaynu, v'chal-k'laynu, v'har-vichaynu, v'harvach lanu, Adonoi Elohaynu, m'hayra mi-kol tzarotaynu, v'na tatz-richaynu, Adonoi Elohaynu, lo li-day matnat basar va-dam, v'lo li-day hal-va-atam, ki im l'yadcha, ha-melaya, ha-petucha, ha-kedosha v'har-chava, she-lo nayvosh, v'lo ni-kalaym l'olam va-ed.*

**God,** our God, have compassion on Israel, Your people, and on Jerusalem, Your city, and on Zion, the place of the Tabernacle of Your honor, and on the kingdom of the house of David, Your messiah, and on our great Holy Temple, upon which Your name is called. Our God, our father, our shepherd, our sustainer, our provider, our supporter, and the One Who brings us relief — bring relief, please, God, our God, quickly, from all our troubles. And please don't make us needy, God, our God, for the handouts of other people, nor for their loans, but only for Your hand, that is full, open, holy, and generous, that we may never be embarrassed or ashamed forever.

God, I'm sitting here in my comfort zone, but I don't want to forget that Jerusalem — Holy Jerusalem — is my city. Even if a Jew has never been there, but especially if he has, Jerusalem is home. I want to use these moments to say, God, thank You for gifting us with that beautiful, ancient, miraculous city that is ours — all of ours. Please be good to Jerusalem. Bless my city with peace and serenity. Rebuild the Temple that used to stand there, so Your presence might be more palpable to us. And as for us, God, the destruction of the Temple brought so many other difficulties in its wake. Because we are distant (in so many ways) from that center of spirituality, we have so many problems. The Jewish People, and the world, is filled with hatred, jealousy, poverty, and other terrible situations.

Please, God, take care of our problems. Nourish us with goodness and love; support us when things are tough; relieve us of our difficulties; clear up our confusion; and give us relief from our troubles. And when it comes to financial distress: open Your generous hand and don't make us rely on other human beings to support us, give us loans, or help us financially. Let us only be reliant on You, as You are so generous with a full heart to give. In this way please let us never feel humiliated or ashamed of our need.

וּבְנֵה יְרוּשָׁלַיִם עִיר הַקֹּדֶשׁ בִּמְהֵרָה בְיָמֵינוּ. בָּרוּךְ אַתָּה יְיָ, בּוֹנֵה בְרַחֲמָיו יְרוּשָׁלָיִם. אָמֵן.

**U-v'nay** *Yerushalayim ir ha-kodesh bim-hayra v'ya-maynu. Baruch Ata Adonoi, bonay v'rachamav Yerushalayim, amen.*

**Build** *Jerusalem, the holy city, quickly and in our days. Blessed are You, God, Who builds Jerusalem with compassion, amen.*

בָּרוּךְ אַתָּה יְיָ אֱלֹהֵינוּ מֶלֶךְ הָעוֹלָם, הָאֵל, אָבִינוּ, מַלְכֵּנוּ, אַדִּירֵנוּ, בּוֹרְאֵנוּ, גּוֹאֲלֵנוּ, יוֹצְרֵנוּ, קְדוֹשֵׁנוּ קְדוֹשׁ יַעֲקֹב, רוֹעֵנוּ רוֹעֵה יִשְׂרָאֵל, הַמֶּלֶךְ הַטּוֹב וְהַמֵּטִיב לַכֹּל, שֶׁבְּכָל יוֹם וָיוֹם הוּא הֵטִיב, הוּא מֵטִיב, הוּא יֵיטִיב לָנוּ. הוּא גְמָלָנוּ, הוּא גוֹמְלֵנוּ, הוּא יִגְמְלֵנוּ לָעַד, לְחֵן וּלְחֶסֶד וּלְרַחֲמִים וּלְרֶוַח הַצָּלָה וְהַצְלָחָה, בְּרָכָה וִישׁוּעָה, נֶחָמָה, פַּרְנָסָה וְכַלְכָּלָה, וְרַחֲמִים וְחַיִּים וְשָׁלוֹם וְכָל טוֹב, וּמִכָּל טוּב לְעוֹלָם אַל יְחַסְּרֵנוּ.

***Baruch*** *Ata Adonoi Elohaynu melech ha-olam, ha-El, avinu, malkaynu, adiraynu, boraynu, go-alaynu, yotzraynu, k'doshaynu, k'dosh Yaakov, ro-aynu, ro-ay Yisrael, ha-melech ha-tov v'ha-maytiv la-kol, she-b'chol yom va-yom hu haytiv, hu maytiv, hu yaytiv lanu; hu g'malanu, hu gom-laynu, hu yig-m'laynu la-ad, l'chayn u-l'chesed u-l'rachamim, u-l'revach hatzala v'hatzlacha bracha; vi-yeshua, nechama, parnasa, v'chalkala, v'rachamim, v'chaim, v'shalom, v'chol tov, u-mi-kol tuv l'olam al y'chas-raynu.*

**Blessed** are You, God, our God, King of the universe, God, our father, our King, our strength, our creator, our redeemer, the One Who fashioned us, the One Who made us holy, the holy One of Jacob, our shepherd — the shepherd of Israel — the good King Who does good to all. For every single day He has done good, continues to do good, and will do good for us; He has given kindness to us, continues to do kindness for us, and will do kindness for us; for grace and for kindness, and for compassion, for relief, salvation, success, blessing, redemption, consolation, livelihood, and support; for compassion, life, peace, and all good — and of all kinds of goodness, never deprive us.

הָרַחֲמָן, הוּא יִמְלוֹךְ עָלֵינוּ לְעוֹלָם וָעֶד.

הָרַחֲמָן, הוּא יִתְבָּרַךְ בַּשָּׁמַיִם וּבָאָרֶץ.

הָרַחֲמָן, הוּא יִשְׁתַּבַּח לְדוֹר דּוֹרִים, וְיִתְפָּאַר בָּנוּ לָעַד וּלְנֵצַח נְצָחִים, וְיִתְהַדַּר בָּנוּ לָעַד וּלְעוֹלְמֵי עוֹלָמִים.

הָרַחֲמָן, הוּא יְפַרְנְסֵנוּ בְּכָבוֹד.

*Gratitude After Eating*

הָרַחֲמָן, הוּא יִשְׁבּוֹר עֻלֵּנוּ מֵעַל צַוָּארֵנוּ וְהוּא יוֹלִיכֵנוּ קוֹמְמִיּוּת לְאַרְצֵנוּ.

הָרַחֲמָן, הוּא יִשְׁלַח לָנוּ בְּרָכָה מְרֻבָּה בַּבַּיִת הַזֶּה, וְעַל שֻׁלְחָן זֶה שֶׁאָכַלְנוּ עָלָיו.

הָרַחֲמָן, הוּא יִשְׁלַח לָנוּ אֶת אֵלִיָּהוּ הַנָּבִיא זָכוּר לַטּוֹב, וִיבַשֶּׂר לָנוּ בְּשׂוֹרוֹת טוֹבוֹת יְשׁוּעוֹת וְנֶחָמוֹת.

**Ha-rachaman** hu yimloch alaynu l'olam va-ed.

**Ha-rachaman** hu yit-barach ba-shamayim u-va-aretz.

**Ha-rachaman** hu yish-tabach l'dor dorim; v'yit-pa-ar banu la-ad u-l'netzach netzachim; v'yit-hadar banu la-ad u-l'olmay olamim.

**Ha-rachaman** hu y'far-n'saynu b'kavod.

**Ha-rachaman** hu yishbor ulaynu may-al tzavaraynu; v'hu yoli-chaynu ko-memiyut l'artzaynu.

**Ha-rachaman** hu yish-lach lanu bracha merubah ba-bayit ha-zeh v'al shulchan zeh she-achalnu alav.

**Ha-rachaman** hu yish-lach lanu et Eliyahu ha-navi zachur la-tov, vi-vaser lanu, besorot tovot, yeshuot v'nechamot.

**May** the compassionate One reign over us forever and ever.

**May** the compassionate One be blessed in heaven and on earth.

**May** the compassionate One be praised for all generations; and may He be glorified through us forever and for all eternity; and may He be beautified through us forever — always and forever.

**May** the compassionate One support us financially with dignity.

**May** the compassionate One break our yoke from upon our necks and lead us upright to our land.

**May** the compassionate One send us abundant blessing to this home, and on this table upon which we've eaten.

**May** the compassionate One send us Elijah the prophet, of blessed memory, and he will report to us good news, salvation, and consolation.

**הָרַחֲמָן**, הוּא יְבָרֵךְ אֶת (אָבִי מוֹרִי) בַּעַל הַבַּיִת הַזֶּה, וְאֶת (אִמִּי מוֹרָתִי) בַּעֲלַת הַבַּיִת הַזֶּה, אוֹתָם וְאֶת בֵּיתָם וְאֶת זַרְעָם וְאֶת כָּל אֲשֶׁר לָהֶם,

**הָרַחֲמָן**, הוּא יְבָרֵךְ אוֹתִי (וְאָבִי | וְאִמִּי | וְאִשְׁתִּי | וְזַרְעִי | וְאֶת כָּל אֲשֶׁר לִי)

**אוֹתָנוּ** וְאֶת כָּל אֲשֶׁר לָנוּ, כְּמוֹ שֶׁנִּתְבָּרְכוּ אֲבוֹתֵינוּ, אַבְרָהָם יִצְחָק וְיַעֲקֹב, בַּכֹּל, מִכֹּל, כֹּל, כֵּן יְבָרֵךְ אוֹתָנוּ כֻּלָּנוּ יַחַד בִּבְרָכָה שְׁלֵמָה, וְנֹאמַר אָמֵן.

**Ha-rachaman** *hu yevarech et*

*[Insert appropriate phrase]:*

*avi mori*

*ba-al ha-bayit ha-zeh [v'et]*

*imi morati*

Gratitude After Eating

ba-alat ha-bayit ha-zeh [v'et]

kol ha-mesubin kan

oti

v'et ba-ali/ishti

v'et zari

v'et kol asher li

otam v'et bay-tam [v'et zar-am] v'et kol asher lahem

otanu v'et kol asher lanu

k'mo she-nit-barchu avotaynu Avraham, Yitzchak, v'Yaakov, ba-kol, mi-kol, kol — kayn yevarech otanu kulanu yachad, bi-vracha she-layma v'nomar amen.

**May** *the compassionate One bless*
[*Insert appropriate phrase*]:

my father, my teacher

the owner of this home [and]

my mother, my teacher

the owner of this home [and]

all those eating here

me

and my husband/wife

and my children

and everything that's mine

they, their homes, [their children] and all that's theirs

us and all that's ours

just as our ancestors were blessed — Abraham, Isaac, and Jacob — with all manners of complete blessing. So may He bless us, all of us together, with a complete blessing, and let us say amen.

בַּמָּרוֹם יְלַמְּדוּ עֲלֵיהֶם וְעָלֵינוּ זְכוּת, שֶׁתְּהֵא לְמִשְׁמֶרֶת שָׁלוֹם, וְנִשָּׂא בְרָכָה מֵאֵת יְיָ, וּצְדָקָה מֵאֱלֹהֵי יִשְׁעֵנוּ, וְנִמְצָא חֵן וְשֵׂכֶל טוֹב בְּעֵינֵי אֱלֹהִים וְאָדָם.

**Ba-marom** y'lamdu alay-hem v'alaynu zechut she-t'hay l'mishmeret shalom, v'nisa v'racha ma-ayt Adonoi, u-tzedaka may-lohay yish-aynu, v'nimtza chayn v'saychel tov b'aynay Elohim v'adam.

**On** high they will learn — for themselves and for us — a merit, that may serve as a preservation of the peace. May we raise up blessing from God, and righteousness from the God of our salvation, and may we find grace and good wisdom in the eyes of God and man.

הָרַחֲמָן, הוּא יְזַכֵּנוּ לִימוֹת הַמָּשִׁיחַ וּלְחַיֵּי הָעוֹלָם הַבָּא. בחול מַגְדִּיל [בשבת ור"ח ויו"ט וחול המועד וראש השנה מִגְדּוֹל] יְשׁוּעוֹת מַלְכּוֹ, וְעֹשֶׂה חֶסֶד לִמְשִׁיחוֹ לְדָוִד וּלְזַרְעוֹ עַד עוֹלָם. עֹשֶׂה שָׁלוֹם בִּמְרוֹמָיו, הוּא יַעֲשֶׂה שָׁלוֹם עָלֵינוּ וְעַל כָּל יִשְׂרָאֵל, וְאִמְרוּ אָמֵן.

יְראוּ אֶת יְיָ קְדֹשָׁיו, כִּי אֵין מַחְסוֹר לִירֵאָיו. כְּפִירִים רָשׁוּ וְרָעֵבוּ, וְדֹרְשֵׁי יְיָ לֹא יַחְסְרוּ כָל טוֹב. הוֹדוּ לַיְיָ כִּי טוֹב, כִּי לְעוֹלָם חַסְדּוֹ. פּוֹתֵחַ אֶת יָדֶךָ, וּמַשְׂבִּיעַ לְכָל חַי רָצוֹן. בָּרוּךְ הַגֶּבֶר אֲשֶׁר יִבְטַח בַּיְיָ, וְהָיָה יְיָ מִבְטַחוֹ. נַעַר הָיִיתִי גַם זָקַנְתִּי,

*Gratitude After Eating*

וְלֹא רָאִיתִי צַדִּיק נֶעֱזָב, וְזַרְעוֹ מְבַקֶּשׁ לָחֶם. יְיָ עֹז לְעַמּוֹ יִתֵּן, יְיָ יְבָרֵךְ אֶת עַמּוֹ בַשָּׁלוֹם.

**Ha-rachaman** hu y'zakaynu li-mot ha-mashiach u-l'chai-ay ha-olam ha-ba. Magdil yeshuot malko v'oseh chesed lim-shicho l'david u-l'zaro ad olam. Oseh shalom bim-romav hu ya-aseh shalom, alaynu v'al kol Yisrael v'imru amen.

**Yiru** et Adonoi k'doshav ki ayn machsor li-rayav, kifirim rashu v'ra-ayvu v'dorshay Adonoi lo yach-s'ru kol tov. Hodu la-Adonoi ki tov, ki l'olam chasdo. Potayach et yadecha, u-mas-biya l'chol chai ratzon. Baruch ha-gever asher yivtach ba-Adonoi v'haya Adonoi miv-tacho. Na-ar hayiti, gam zakan-ti, v'lo ra-iti tzadik ne-ezav, v'zaro mevakesh lachem. Adonoi oz l'amo yi-tayn, Adonoi yivarech, et amo ba-shalom.

**May** the compassionate One make us worthy to merit the days of the Messiah, and to the life of the world to come. He makes great the salvations of His king, and does kindness for His Messiah, for David and his descendants, forever. He Who makes peace on high, may He create peace upon us and all of Israel — and let us say amen. Revere God, His holy ones, for those that revere Him will never lack. Young lions may be deprived and hungry — but those that seek God will not lack for anything. Give praise to God for He is good — for His kindness lasts forever. Open Your hand, and satisfy the desire of all living things. Blessed is the man who *relies on God, and may God be his mainstay. I was a young man, and now I've grown old, and I've never seen a righteous person left abandoned, with his children begging for bread. God is strong enough to provide for His nation; God will bless His nation with peace.*

*Part Three:*

# SHABBAT

# Prayer on Challah Baking

The mitzvah of challah baking is one of the three mitzvot designated for women. During Temple times, every time a woman baked, she'd remove a small amount to donate to the kohain (Jewish priest). In modern times, we too take off a small amount, and although we no longer know with certainty who is of the priestly family, this is a mitzvah of honoring them and remembering that enjoying our bounty must include gratitude to God and sharing with others.

As with any special mitzvah such as candlelighting, the moments immediately following the mitzvah are a time of Divine favor in which one should pray for all that is on her mind, and include mention of one's family members, friends, and others whose needs might include healing, the blessing of a soulmate or children, help at a difficult time of life, or any other need.

Ironically, the small piece that is removed is actually called "challah," and the rest of the batch is simply called bread. Nevertheless, we now call these loaves baked for use on Shabbat and holidays "challah" in commemoration of the mitzvah done through them.

**When baking a batch of 5 lbs. of flour or more, a small handful is removed and the following blessing is said.**
**If the amount is 2 ½ lb–5 lb. the piece is separated without a blessing. A batch smaller than 2 ½ lb. of flour is not included in this mitzvah.**

בָּרוּךְ אַתָּה יְיָ אֱלֹהֵינוּ מֶלֶךְ הָעוֹלָם, אֲשֶׁר קִדְּשָׁנוּ בְּמִצְוֹתָיו וְצִוָּנוּ לְהַפְרִישׁ חַלָּה מִן הָעִסָּה׃

**Baruch** ata Adonoi, Elohaynu melech ha-olam, asher kid-shanu b'mitzvotav, v'tzivanu l'hafrish challah min ha-isah.

**Blessed** are You, God, our God, King of the universe, Who has made us holy with His commandments, and commanded us to separate the "challah" from the dough.

The small piece of dough is now discarded — either by completely burning it through and through so that it is no longer edible; or by double-wrapping it and discarding.

**May** it be Your will, God and the God of our ancestors, that the mitzvah of separating challah be considered as though I fulfilled it the optimal way as in the times of the Temple. Please consider it as a personal sacrifice from me, and just as sacrifices in Temple times atoned for all misdeeds, may this mitzvah be an atonement for me, for my mistakes and misdeeds. Please allow me to celebrate Shabbat and holidays [with my husband, children, parents] and be nourished by the holiness of this mitzvah. [May my children be influenced by the holiness that this mitzvah introduces into our home and] may we all be sustained by You in mercy, kindness, and love. Just as I participated in this mitzvah wholeheartedly, may You wholeheartedly have compassion on us, to always shield us from suffering and pain. Amen. [Mention any specific prayers here for individuals.]

# Candlelighting for Shabbat and Holidays

The lighting of the candles, along with using the mikveh and separating challah, is one of the traditions uniquely given to women. Lighting candles at the onset of Shabbat is meant to bring more light and peace into the world — literally and mystically. Women are generally instinctively talented in this arena. The moments after performing these three mitzvot are considered a time of Divine favor during which to pray from the heart for whatever is uppermost in our minds.

**Instructions:** Light two candles (some have a custom to light an additional candle for each child) prior to sunset. Wave your hands in a circular motion to "wave in" the spirit of Shabbat. Cover your eyes briefly, then say:

FOR SHABBAT:

בָּרוּךְ אַתָּה יְיָ אֱלֹהֵינוּ מֶלֶךְ הָעוֹלָם, אֲשֶׁר קִדְּשָׁנוּ בְּמִצְוֹתָיו, וְצִוָּנוּ לְהַדְלִיק נֵר שֶׁל שַׁבָּת.

**Baruch** ata Adonoi, Elohaynu melech ha-olam, asher kid-shanu b'mitzvotav, v'tzivanu l'hadlik ner shel Shabbat.

**Blessed** are You, God, our God, King of the universe, Who has sanctified us with His commandments, and commanded us to light the candles of Shabbat.

FOR ROSH HASHANAH AND OTHER HOLIDAYS (ADD BRACKETED PHRASE WHEN IT COINCIDES WITH SHABBAT):

בָּרוּךְ אַתָּה יְיָ אֱלֹהֵינוּ מֶלֶךְ הָעוֹלָם, אֲשֶׁר קִדְּשָׁנוּ בְּמִצְוֹתָיו, וְצִוָּנוּ לְהַדְלִיק נֵר שֶׁל (שַׁבָּת וְשֶׁל) יוֹם טוֹב.

**Baruch** ata Adonoi, Elohaynu melech ha-olam, asher kid-shanu b'mitzvotav, v'tzivanu l'hadlik ner shel [Shabbat v'shel] Yom Tov.

**Blessed** are You, God, our God, King of the universe, Who has sanctified us with His commandments, and

*Shabbat*

commanded us to light the candles of [Shabbat and] the holiday.

FOR YOM KIPPUR:

בָּרוּךְ אַתָּה יְיָ אֱלֹהֵינוּ מֶלֶךְ הָעוֹלָם, אֲשֶׁר קִדְּשָׁנוּ בְּמִצְוֹתָיו וְצִוָּנוּ לְהַדְלִיק נֵר שֶׁל (שַׁבָּת וְשֶׁל) יוֹם הַכִּפּוּרִים.

**Baruch** ata Adonoi, Elohaynu melech ha-olam, asher kid-shanu b'mitzvotav, v'tzivanu l'hadlik ner shel [Shabbat v'shel] Yom Hakippurim.

**Blessed** are You, God, our God, King of the universe, Who has sanctified us with His commandments, and commanded us to light the candles of [Shabbat and] Yom Kippur.

ADD ON HOLIDAYS AND YOM KIPPUR:

בָּרוּךְ אַתָּה יְיָ אֱלֹהֵינוּ מֶלֶךְ הָעוֹלָם, שֶׁהֶחֱיָנוּ וְקִיְּמָנוּ וְהִגִּיעָנוּ לַזְּמַן הַזֶּה.

**Baruch** ata Adonoi, Elohaynu melech ha-olam, she-he-che-yanu, v'kee-manu, v'hee-geeyanu la-zman ha-zeh.

**Blessed** *are You, God, our God, King of the universe, Who has kept us alive, and sustained us, and allowed us to reach this season.*

יְ**הִי** רָצוֹן לְפָנֶיךָ, יְיָ אֱלֹהַי וֵאלֹהֵי אֲבוֹתַי, שֶׁתְּחוֹנֵן אוֹתִי [וְאֶת אִישִׁי, וְאֶת בָּנַי, וְאֶת בְּנוֹתַי] וְאֶת כָּל קְרוֹבַי, וְתִתֵּן לָנוּ וּלְכָל יִשְׂרָאֵל חַיִּים טוֹבִים וַאֲרוּכִים, וְתִזְכְּרֵנוּ בְּזִכְרוֹן טוֹבָה וּבְרָכָה, וְתִפְקְדֵנוּ בִּפְקֻדַּת יְשׁוּעָה וְרַחֲמִים, וּתְבָרְכֵנוּ בְּרָכוֹת גְּדוֹלוֹת, וְתַשְׁלִים בָּתֵּינוּ, וְתַשְׁכֵּן שְׁכִינָתְךָ בֵּינֵינוּ. וְזַכֵּנִי לְגַדֵּל בָּנִים וּבְנֵי בָנִים חֲכָמִים וּנְבוֹנִים, אוֹהֲבֵי יְיָ, יִרְאֵי אֱלֹהִים, אַנְשֵׁי אֱמֶת, זֶרַע קֹדֶשׁ, בַּיְיָ דְּבֵקִים, וּמְאִירִים אֶת הָעוֹלָם בַּתּוֹרָה וּבְמַעֲשִׂים טוֹבִים, וּבְכָל מְלֶאכֶת עֲבוֹדַת הַבּוֹרֵא. אָנָּא שְׁמַע אֶת תְּחִנָּתִי בָּעֵת הַזֹּאת, בִּזְכוּת שָׂרָה וְרִבְקָה וְרָחֵל וְלֵאָה אִמּוֹתֵינוּ, וְהָאֵר נֵרֵנוּ שֶׁלֹּא יִכְבֶּה לְעוֹלָם וָעֶד, וְהָאֵר פָּנֶיךָ וְנִוָּשֵׁעָה. אָמֵן.

**Ye-hi** ratzon mil-fanecha, Adonoi Elohai vAy-lohay Yisrael she-tichonayn oti (v'et ishi, v'et banai v'et b'no-tai) v'et kol kro-vai, v'titayn lanu u-l'chol Yisrael chaim tovim va-aruchim, v'tiz-k'raynu b'zichron tova u-v'racha, v'tif-kidaynu b'fekudat yeshua v'rachamim, u-t'var-chaynu brachot g'dolot, v'tashlim ba-taynu, v'tash-kayn sh'chinat-cha bay-naynu v'zakaynu l'gadel banim u-v'nay vanim chachamim u-n'vonim, oha-vay Adonoi, yiray Elohim, anshay emet, zera kodesh ba-Adonay d'vay-kim, u-me'irim et ha-olam ba-Torah

*Shabbat* 121

*u-v'ma'asim tovim u-v'chol m'lechet avodat ha-boray. Ana, shema et t'chinati ba-ayt ha-zot bi-z'chut Sara, v'Rivka, v'Rachel, v'Leah imo-taynu, v'ha-er nay-raynu shelo yich-beh l'olam va-ed, v'ha-er panecha v'niva-shaya, amen.*

Dear God,

Thank You for the gift of Shabbat. Thank You for this opportunity to pause in a crazy whirlwind of a week and focus on what's really important: family, friends, and faith. And thank You for the opportunity to light these candles to usher in the beauty and serenity of Shabbat. As the woman of the home I know it's my special opportunity to create peace in this home. I bring light into this home in many ways, and these candles show just that. As I light them, and fulfill my special mitzvah, I know, God, that it's a weekly time of Divine favor, and I intend to fully use these moments to talk to You about the things that are most important. It's amazing that no matter what is going on, every week Shabbat comes, and every week I can take these moments to light the candles and talk to You about what's on my mind most. So here goes.

---

THANK YOU FOR THIS OPPORTUNITY TO PAUSE IN A CRAZY WHIRLWIND OF A WEEK AND FOCUS ON WHAT'S REALLY IMPORTANT: FAMILY, FRIENDS, AND FAITH.

---

God, please shine Your special grace on me [add applicable: on my husband, my sons/daughters, parents, add anyone special by name]. Give us long and happy lives, remember us well when You are making important decisions about our lives, be compassionate with us, and send us lots of blessings and goodness. I want Your presence to shine in this home, so it can be a home of goodness, of love, warmth, and caring — a home where the members of this family are good to one another and always feel safe and loved, and a home where others are welcome and enjoy coming.

Please allow us to have/raise children and grandchildren who are good, happy, and wise; who understand Who You are and know that they can always talk to You, who are truthful and honest, and who will go out into the world as adults and role models and shining examples of humanity and of the Jewish people.

---

[INSERT PERSONAL REQUESTS FOR OTHERS HERE: FOR HEALING, TO FIND A MARRIAGE PARTNER, TO FIND A JOB, OR FOR ANY DIFFICULTY.]

---

Please, God, hear my words at this time — I'm not only asking for all these things just for my merit, but there are many great people who came before me. (Add treasured departed family members here by name) in addition to our great Patriarchs and Matriarchs in Jewish history such as Abraham, Isaac, Jacob, Sarah, Rebecca, Rachel, and Leah, who were so spiritual and great. I am their descendant! So please, for them if not for me, hear my words and listen as I ask of You for all the things that are so important to me. Amen, and Shabbat Shalom.

## Shalom Aleichem

*Shalom Aleichem is a beautiful hymn that is traditionally sung on Friday nights, ideally upon returning from synagogue. Tradition teaches that there are special angels of Shabbat that enter our homes and look around. If the table and family are prepared to greet Shabbat, the "good" angel blesses, "May it be so next week as well!" And the "bad" angel is compelled to reply, "Amen!" But if all is in disarray and no one is greeting Shabbat, the "bad" angel says, "So may it be next week!" and the "good" angel must reply, against its will, "Amen." We welcome the angels, ask them to bless us, and bid them farewell. Some have the custom of singing each verse three times.*

שָׁלוֹם עֲלֵיכֶם, מַלְאֲכֵי הַשָּׁרֵת, מַלְאֲכֵי עֶלְיוֹן, מִמֶּלֶךְ מַלְכֵי הַמְּלָכִים, הַקָּדוֹשׁ בָּרוּךְ הוּא.

*Shabbat*

***Shalom*** *aleichem, malachay ha-sharet, malachay elyon, mi-melech malchay ha-m'lachim, ha-Kadosh Baruch Hu.*

***Peace*** *be upon you, ministering angels, angels on high, from the King of all kings, the Holy One, blessed is He.*

בּוֹאֲכֶם לְשָׁלוֹם, מַלְאֲכֵי הַשָּׁלוֹם, מַלְאֲכֵי עֶלְיוֹן, מִמֶּלֶךְ מַלְכֵי הַמְּלָכִים, הַקָּדוֹשׁ בָּרוּךְ הוּא.

***Bo-achem*** *l'shalom, malachay ha-shalom, malachay elyon, mi-melech malchay ha-m'lachim, ha-Kadosh Baruch Hu.*

***Come*** *in peace, angels of peace, angels on high, from the King of all kings, the Holy One, blessed is He.*

בָּרְכוּנִי לְשָׁלוֹם, מַלְאֲכֵי הַשָּׁלוֹם, מַלְאֲכֵי עֶלְיוֹן, מִמֶּלֶךְ מַלְכֵי הַמְּלָכִים, הַקָּדוֹשׁ בָּרוּךְ הוּא.

***Bar-chuni*** *l'shalom, malachay ha-shalom, malachay elyon, mi-melech malchay ha-m'lachim, ha-Kadosh Baruch Hu.*

***Bless*** *us in peace, angels of peace, angels on high, from the King of all kings, the Holy One, blessed is He.*

צֵאתְכֶם לְשָׁלוֹם, מַלְאֲכֵי הַשָּׁלוֹם, מַלְאֲכֵי עֶלְיוֹן, מִמֶּלֶךְ מַלְכֵי הַמְּלָכִים, הַקָּדוֹשׁ בָּרוּךְ הוּא.

***Tzayt-chem*** *l'shalom, malachay ha-shalom, malachay elyon, mi-melech malchay ha-m'lachim, Ha-kadosh Baruch Hu.*

**Go** out in peace, angels of peace, angels on high, from the King of all kings, the Holy One, blessed is He.

# Aishet Chayil

Aishet Chayil is a beautiful poem that was originally composed by our patriarch Abraham as a eulogy for his wife, Sarah. It is arranged according to the letters of the Hebrew alphabet, with one accolade for each letter. The poem was later included by King Solomon in his Book of Proverbs. In it is described the wonderful attributes of a Jewish woman, and it is customary for Jewish men to sing it to their wives each Friday night at dinner

אֵשֶׁת חַיִל מִי יִמְצָא, וְרָחֹק מִפְּנִינִים מִכְרָהּ.

בָּטַח בָּהּ לֵב בַּעְלָהּ, וְשָׁלָל לֹא יֶחְסָר.

גְּמָלַתְהוּ טוֹב וְלֹא רָע, כֹּל יְמֵי חַיֶּיהָ.

דָּרְשָׁה צֶמֶר וּפִשְׁתִּים, וַתַּעַשׂ בְּחֵפֶץ כַּפֶּיהָ.

הָיְתָה כָּאֳנִיּוֹת סוֹחֵר, מִמֶּרְחָק תָּבִיא לַחְמָהּ.

וַתָּקָם בְּעוֹד לַיְלָה, וַתִּתֵּן טֶרֶף לְבֵיתָהּ, וְחֹק לְנַעֲרֹתֶיהָ.

זָמְמָה שָׂדֶה וַתִּקָּחֵהוּ, מִפְּרִי כַפֶּיהָ נָטְעָה כָּרֶם.

חָגְרָה בְעוֹז מָתְנֶיהָ, וַתְּאַמֵּץ זְרוֹעֹתֶיהָ.

טָעֲמָה כִּי טוֹב סַחְרָהּ, לֹא יִכְבֶּה בַלַּיְלָה נֵרָהּ.

יָדֶיהָ שִׁלְּחָה בַכִּישׁוֹר, וְכַפֶּיהָ תָּמְכוּ פָלֶךְ.

כַּפָּהּ פָּרְשָׂה לֶעָנִי, וְיָדֶיהָ שִׁלְּחָה לָאֶבְיוֹן.

*Shabbat*

**לֹא** תִירָא לְבֵיתָהּ מִשָּׁלֶג, כִּי כָל בֵּיתָהּ לָבֻשׁ שָׁנִים.

**מַ**רְבַדִּים עָשְׂתָה לָּהּ, שֵׁשׁ וְאַרְגָּמָן לְבוּשָׁהּ.

**נ**וֹדָע בַּשְּׁעָרִים בַּעְלָהּ, בְּשִׁבְתּוֹ עִם זִקְנֵי אָרֶץ.

**סָ**דִין עָשְׂתָה וַתִּמְכֹּר, וַחֲגוֹר נָתְנָה לַכְּנַעֲנִי.

**ע**ֹז וְהָדָר לְבוּשָׁהּ, וַתִּשְׂחַק לְיוֹם אַחֲרוֹן.

**פִּ**יהָ פָּתְחָה בְחָכְמָה, וְתוֹרַת חֶסֶד עַל לְשׁוֹנָהּ.

**צ**וֹפִיָּה הֲלִיכוֹת בֵּיתָהּ, וְלֶחֶם עַצְלוּת לֹא תֹאכֵל.

**קָ**מוּ בָנֶיהָ וַיְאַשְּׁרוּהָ, בַּעְלָהּ וַיְהַלְלָהּ.

**רַ**בּוֹת בָּנוֹת עָשׂוּ חָיִל, וְאַתְּ עָלִית עַל כֻּלָּנָה.

**שֶׁ**קֶר הַחֵן וְהֶבֶל הַיֹּפִי, אִשָּׁה יִרְאַת יְיָ הִיא תִתְהַלָּל.

**תְּ**נוּ לָהּ מִפְּרִי יָדֶיהָ, וִיהַלְלוּהָ בַשְּׁעָרִים מַעֲשֶׂיהָ.

**Aishet** chayil mi yimtza, v'rachok mi-peninim michra.

Batach ba lev ba-ala, v'shalal lo yech-sar.

G'malat-hu tov v'lo ra, kol y'may chai-yeha.

Darsha tzemer u-fish-tim, va-ta-as b'che-fetz kapeha.

Hayta ka-aniyat socher, mi-merchak tavi lachma.

Va-takam b'od laila, va-titayn teref l'bayta v'chok l'na-aroteha.

Zam'ma sadeh va-tikachehu, mi-pri kapeha nata karem.

Chagra b'oz mat-neha va-t'ametz z'ro-o-teha.

Ta-ama ki tov sachra, lo yich-beh ba-laila nayra.

Yadeha shil-cha ba-kishor, v'kapeha tam-chu palech.

*Kapa parsa le-ani v'yadeha shilcha la-evyon.*

*Lo tira l'vayta mi-shaleg, ki chol vayta lavush shanim.*

*Marvadim as'ta la, shesh v'argaman le'vusha.*

*Noda ba-sh'arim ba-ala, b'shivto im ziknay aretz.*

*Sadin as'ta va-timkor v'chagor natna la-kenani.*

*Oz v'hadar levusha, va-tis-chak l'yom acharon.*

*Piha patcha b'chochma, v'torat chesed al leshona.*

*Tzofi-ha halichot bayta, v'lechem atzlut lo to-chel.*

*Kamu baneha vaya-shru-ha ba-ala vai-y'halela.*

*Rabot banot asu chayil, v'at aleet al kulana.*

*Sheker ha-chen v'hevel ha-yofi, isha yirat Adonoi, hi tit-halal.*

*T'nu la mipri yadeha vi-ha-leluha ba-shearim ma-aseha.*

**A woman** of valor who can find? Her worth is beyond pearls.

Her husband's heart trusts her and he never lacks for fortune.

She does good for him and not bad all the days of her life.

She seeks out wool and linen, and willingly creates with her hands.

She is like a merchant ship, she brings bread from afar.

She gets up while it's still night and brings food for her household and gives her servants the rules.

She surveys a field and buys it; through her hands, the vineyards are planted.

*Her limbs are prepared to work and are strengthened, and she strengthens her bones.*

*She perceives that her merchandise is good; her candle doesn't go out at night.*

*Her hand is stretched out to the spinning stick, and her palms support the spindle.*

*Her palm is outstretched to the needy, and her hand she sends out to the destitute.*

*Her home need not worry about snow, for her whole household is dressed in wools of red.*

*She makes for herself beautiful linens, her clothing is linen and purple wool.*

*Her husband is well-known at the city gates, as he sits with the elders of the community.*

*She makes bed linen and sells them, and she donates her belt to the peddler.*

*Her clothing is strong and honorable, and she can laugh at her last day.*

*Her mouth is open with wisdom, and the Torah of kindness is on her tongue.*

*She anticipates the ways of her home, and never eats the bread of laziness.*

*Her children get up and praise her; her husband, and he glorifies her.*

*Many women have done valorous deeds, but you have surpassed them all.*

*Physical grace is false, and external beauty is nothing, but a woman who reveres God is the one to be praised.*

*Give her the rewards of her hands, and may her deeds be praised at the city gates.*

# Kiddush

Kiddush is recited at the onset of Shabbat dinner. A full cup of wine or grape juice is used. Everyone should enjoy a sip of the Kiddush wine or grape juice after responding "amen."

וַיְהִי עֶרֶב וַיְהִי בֹקֶר

**יוֹם** הַשִּׁשִּׁי. וַיְכֻלּוּ הַשָּׁמַיִם וְהָאָרֶץ וְכָל צְבָאָם. וַיְכַל אֱלֹהִים בַּיּוֹם הַשְּׁבִיעִי מְלַאכְתּוֹ אֲשֶׁר עָשָׂה, וַיִּשְׁבֹּת בַּיּוֹם הַשְּׁבִיעִי, מִכָּל מְלַאכְתּוֹ אֲשֶׁר עָשָׂה. וַיְבָרֶךְ אֱלֹהִים אֶת יוֹם הַשְּׁבִיעִי וַיְקַדֵּשׁ אֹתוֹ, כִּי בוֹ שָׁבַת מִכָּל מְלַאכְתּוֹ, אֲשֶׁר בָּרָא אֱלֹהִים לַעֲשׂוֹת.

**בָּרוּךְ** אַתָּה יְיָ אֱלֹהֵינוּ מֶלֶךְ הָעוֹלָם, בּוֹרֵא פְּרִי הַגָּפֶן.

**בָּרוּךְ** אַתָּה יְיָ אֱלֹהֵינוּ מֶלֶךְ הָעוֹלָם, אֲשֶׁר קִדְּשָׁנוּ בְּמִצְוֹתָיו וְרָצָה בָנוּ, וְשַׁבַּת קָדְשׁוֹ בְּאַהֲבָה וּבְרָצוֹן הִנְחִילָנוּ זִכָּרוֹן לְמַעֲשֵׂה בְרֵאשִׁית, כִּי הוּא יוֹם תְּחִלָּה לְמִקְרָאֵי קֹדֶשׁ, זֵכֶר לִיצִיאַת מִצְרָיִם, כִּי בָנוּ בָחַרְתָּ וְאוֹתָנוּ קִדַּשְׁתָּ מִכָּל הָעַמִּים, וְשַׁבַּת קָדְשְׁךָ בְּאַהֲבָה וּבְרָצוֹן הִנְחַלְתָּנוּ. בָּרוּךְ אַתָּה יְיָ, מְקַדֵּשׁ הַשַּׁבָּת.

**Va-y'hi** erev vay-y'hi voker yom ha-shishi. Va-y'chulu ha-shamayim v'ha-aretz v'chol tz'va-am.

*Shabbat*

*Va-y'chal Elohim ba-yom ha-shvi-i melach-to asher asa. Va-yish-bot ba-yom ha-shvi-i mi-kol melachto asher asa. Va-y'varech Elohim et yom ha-shvi-i va-y'kadesh oto, ki vo shavat mi-kol melachto asher bara Elohim la-asot.*

**Savri,** *baruch Ata Adonoi, Elohaynu melech ha-olam, boray pri ha-gafen.*

**Baruch** *Ata Adonoi, Elohaynu melech ha-olam, asher kid-shanu b'mitzvotav v'ratza vanu, v'Shabbat kadsho b'ahava u-v'ratzon hin-chilanu, zikaron l'ma-aseh v'ray-sheet. Ki hu yom techilah l'mikra-ay kodesh, zecher li-yitzi-at mitzrayim. Ki vanu vacharta v'otanu kidashta mi-kol ha-amim, v'Shabbat kadsh'cha b'ahava u-v'ratzon hin-chal-tanu. Baruch Ata Adonoi, mekadesh ha-Shabbat.*

**"And** it was evening, and it was morning, the sixth day. And the heavens and earth were finished, and all their hosts. And God finished on the seventh day all the creative work that He had made. And He rested on the seventh day from all the creative work He had made. And God blessed the seventh day and made it holy, because on it, He rested from all the creative work that God created to make" (Genesis 1:31-2:3).

**Blessed** are You, God, our God, King of the universe, Who has made the fruit of the vine.

**Blessed** are You, God, our God, King of the universe, Who has made us holy with His commandments and favored us, and Your holy Sabbath, with love and *favor You have bequeathed to us as a memorial to the works of Creation. For it is the very beginning of the holy days — a memorial of our Exodus from Egypt. For You have chosen us and sanctified us from all the nations, and Your holy Shabbat, with love and favor, You've bequeathed to us. Blessed are You, God, Who has sanctified the Sabbath.*

God, when we lift up a cup of grape juice or wine, we demonstrate that every physical item in this world can be elevated for spirituality. On Shabbat we celebrate the fact that You created this physical world and everything in it, and all You ask is that we remember its source and use the blessings in it for goodness and spirituality. We declare on Shabbat that the entire world and everything in it is Yours, and that we use it all week and step back on Shabbat — to remember what it's all about and use it for a higher purpose. Thank You, God, for the gift of Shabbat on which to sanctify and elevate our lives.

---

WE DECLARE ON SHABBAT THAT THE ENTIRE WORLD AND EVERYTHING IN IT IS YOURS, AND THAT WE USE IT ALL WEEK AND STEP BACK ON SHABBAT — TO REMEMBER WHAT IT'S ALL ABOUT AND USE IT FOR A HIGHER PURPOSE.

---

# Handwashing

We wash our hands for bread to show that eating a meal can bring holiness into our daily lives. Just as the Jewish priests in ancient times washed their hands ritually before the Temple service, we too wash our hands in the temples of our own homes in preparation for meal time.

*Shabbat*

Remove your rings so that the water touches all parts of your hands. Pour water twice over your right hand, then twice over your left. Use plenty of water — it's an omen for wealth! Say the blessing.

בָּרוּךְ אַתָּה יְיָ אֱלֹהֵינוּ מֶלֶךְ הָעוֹלָם אֲשֶׁר קִדְּשָׁנוּ בְּמִצְוֹתָיו, וְצִוָּנוּ עַל נְטִילַת יָדָיִם.

**Baruch** Ata Adonoi, Elohaynu melech ha-olam, asher kidshanu b'mitzvotav, v'tzeevanu al n'tilat yadayim.

**Blessed** are You, God, our God, King of the universe, Who has sanctified us with His commandments, and commanded us to wash our hands.

Now the hard part: we don't talk until we say "Hamotzi" and taste the bread. Good luck!

# Hamotzi

בָּרוּךְ אַתָּה יְיָ אֱלֹהֵינוּ מֶלֶךְ הָעוֹלָם הַמּוֹצִיא לֶחֶם מִן הָאָרֶץ.

**Baruch** Ata Adonoi, Elohaynu melech ha-olam, hamotzi lechem min ha-aretz.

**Blessed** are You, God, our God, King of the universe, Who has brought forth bread from the earth.

God, thank You for bringing bread from the earth. Thank You for letting us partner with You — You created the raw materials of nature, and the science to allow us to turn it into something delicious. You gifted us with wisdom to turn wheat into bread, and the ability to be grateful for it! Thank You!

# Shabbat Amidah

*The Amidah is the centerpiece of the prayer. It literally means "standing," as it is recited while standing. The Amidah should be said at a time and place where a person will not be disturbed. One should not interrupt to speak of other things in the middle of any prayer — but this is especially true of the Amidah. While praying the Amidah, one should face east, toward Israel (or whichever direction is toward Israel for the one praying). One should stand with feet together and not move the feet until completion. One should try to truly envision standing before our kind and benevolent God, Who is just waiting to hear from us. One should pray the Amidah in a whisper or undertone. This is between you and God.*

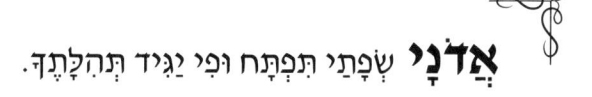

אֲדֹנָי שְׂפָתַי תִּפְתָּח וּפִי יַגִּיד תְּהִלָּתֶךָ.

**Adonoi** *sfa-tai tiftach, u-fi yagid tehilatecha.*

**My** Lord, open my lips, and may my mouth speak Your praises.

Dear God,
I stand here before You, ready to share my thoughts and reflections with You. It's intimidating, and I don't want to do it wrong! But I'm just going to start... I know You'll understand.

## ANCESTORS

*Bow at the beginning and end of this blessing.*

*Shabbat*

בָּרוּךְ אַתָּה יְיָ אֱלֹהֵינוּ וֵאלֹהֵי אֲבוֹתֵינוּ, אֱלֹהֵי אַבְרָהָם, אֱלֹהֵי יִצְחָק, וֵאלֹהֵי יַעֲקֹב, הָאֵל הַגָּדוֹל הַגִּבּוֹר וְהַנּוֹרָא, אֵל עֶלְיוֹן, גּוֹמֵל חֲסָדִים טוֹבִים, וְקֹנֵה הַכֹּל, וְזוֹכֵר חַסְדֵי אָבוֹת, וּמֵבִיא גוֹאֵל לִבְנֵי בְנֵיהֶם, לְמַעַן שְׁמוֹ בְּאַהֲבָה. מֶלֶךְ עוֹזֵר וּמוֹשִׁיעַ וּמָגֵן. בָּרוּךְ אַתָּה יְיָ, מָגֵן אַבְרָהָם.

**Baruch** Ata Adonoi, Elohaynu vay-lohay avotaynu, Elohay Avraham, Elohay Yitzchok, vay-lohay Yaakov. Ha-El ha-gadol ha-gibor v'ha-nora El elyon, go-mel chasadim tovim, v'konay ha-kol, v'zocher chasday avot, u-may-vi go-el liv-nay v'nayhem, l'ma-an sh'mo b'ahava. Melech ozer u-moshiya u-magen. Baruch Ata Adonoi, magen Avraham.

**Blessed** are You, God, our God, and the God of our ancestors, God of Abraham, God of Isaac, God of Jacob. The great, strong, and awesome God; exalted God, Who bestows good kindnesses, owns everything, remembers the kindness of our ancestors, and brings a redeemer to their grandchildren, for the sake of His name, with love. King, helper, savior and shield. Blessed are You, God, shield of Abraham.

The first thing I'd like to do, God, is acknowledge that while I think I'm a pretty good person overall, I do often forget that You are the source of everything in my life. Fortunately, God, I have our Jewish role models, Abraham, Isaac, and Jacob, who came before us, who did not take that gift for granted. They were so loyal to You, and please remember on this important day that I am one of their children. Be kind to me for their sakes - if not for my own.

# GOD'S STRENGTH

אַתָּה גִּבּוֹר לְעוֹלָם אֲדֹנָי, מְחַיֵּה מֵתִים אַתָּה, רַב לְהוֹשִׁיעַ. (בחורף: מַשִּׁיב הָרוּחַ וּמוֹרִיד הַגֶּשֶׁם.) מְכַלְכֵּל חַיִּים בְּחֶסֶד, מְחַיֵּה מֵתִים בְּרַחֲמִים רַבִּים, סוֹמֵךְ נוֹפְלִים, וְרוֹפֵא חוֹלִים, וּמַתִּיר אֲסוּרִים, וּמְקַיֵּם אֱמוּנָתוֹ לִישֵׁנֵי עָפָר, מִי כָמוֹךָ בַּעַל גְּבוּרוֹת וּמִי דוֹמֶה לָךְ, מֶלֶךְ מֵמִית וּמְחַיֶּה וּמַצְמִיחַ יְשׁוּעָה. וְנֶאֱמָן אַתָּה לְהַחֲיוֹת מֵתִים. בָּרוּךְ אַתָּה יְיָ, מְחַיֵּה הַמֵּתִים.

***Ata*** *gibor l'olam Adonoi, mechayeh may-tim Ata rav l'hoshiya.* [In winter: Mashiv ha-ruach u-morid ha-gashem.] *Mechalkel chaim b'chesed, m'chayeh maytim b'rachamim rabim. Somech noflim v'rofay cholim, u-matir asurim, u-m'kayem emunato li-shaynay afar. Mi chamocha ba-al gevurot u-mi domeh lach, melech may-mit u-m'chayeh, u-matz-miyach yeshua. V'ne-eman Ata l'hachayot may-tim. Baruch Ata Adonoi, m'chayeh ha-maytim.*

***You*** *are eternally strong, God. You revive the dead and save abundantly.* [In winter: **You blow the wind and bring down the rain.**] *You sustain the living ones with kindness; You revive the dead with great compassion. You support the fallen, heal the sick, release the bound, and keep Your promise to those that are already resting in the dust. Who is like You, master of strengths? Who can compare to You? You are the King Who brings death and restores life and plants the seeds of redemption. You are trustworthy to revive the dead. Blessed are You, God, Who revives the dead.*

*Shabbat*

God, I acknowledge that You are the source of life and death. Sometimes we get distracted by all the other "causes" — but I affirm that life and death are in Your hands. No one else has that power.

## HOLINESS

אַ**תָּה** קָדוֹשׁ וְשִׁמְךָ קָדוֹשׁ, וּקְדוֹשִׁים בְּכָל יוֹם יְהַלְלוּךָ סֶּלָה. בָּרוּךְ אַתָּה יְיָ, הָאֵל הַקָּדוֹשׁ.

***Ata*** *kadosh v'shimcha kadosh u-kedoshim b'chol yom y'halelucha selah. Baruch Ata Adonoi, ha-El ha-kadosh.*

***You*** *are holy and Your name is holy, and holy ones praise You daily. Blessed are You, God, the holy God.*

God, as I stand here before You, I need to take a minute to focus on Who You actually are. How is it that the most powerful Being in the world is available to me, 24/7? You handle the weather. You keep us alive every day. You are so compassionate. You support me when I fall. You heal the sick. And You keep Your promises to those that are long gone. Who else is like that? And although I am not so well-versed in "holiness," God, if anyone is holy, it's You. Sometimes I meet people, or places that feel "holy" — it's because they contain a spark of You. You are a source of that.

## KEDUSHA

*Kedusha is a part of the repetition of the Amidah by the chazzan only where a minyan is present. It recalls the angelic service and praise of God and is often recited with turn-taking by congregation and cantor, incorporating haunting and beautiful tunes. The verses in quotes are words from Isaiah, Ezekiel, and Psalms.*

*Congregation, repeated by cantor:*

**נְקַדֵּשׁ** אֶת שִׁמְךָ בָּעוֹלָם, כְּשֵׁם שֶׁמַּקְדִּישִׁים אוֹתוֹ בִּשְׁמֵי מָרוֹם, כַּכָּתוּב עַל יַד נְבִיאֶךָ, וְקָרָא זֶה אֶל זֶה וְאָמַר:

***N'kadesh*** *et shimchah ba-olam k'shem she-mak-dishim oto bish-may marom, ka-katuv al yad n'vi-echa v'kara zeh el zeh v'amar.*

**We** will sanctify Your name in this world, just as [the angels] sanctify it in the highest heavens, as it is said via our prophets, "And [the angels] called to one another, and said:"

*Congregation, repeated by cantor:*

**קָדוֹשׁ**, קָדוֹשׁ, קָדוֹשׁ, יְיָ צְבָאוֹת, מְלֹא כָל הָאָרֶץ כְּבוֹדוֹ. אָז בְּקוֹל רַעַשׁ גָּדוֹל אַדִּיר וְחָזָק, מַשְׁמִיעִים קוֹל, מִתְנַשְּׂאִים לְעֻמַּת שְׂרָפִים, לְעֻמָּתָם בָּרוּךְ יֹאמֵרוּ:

***Kadosh,*** *kadosh, kadosh, Adonoi tz'va-ot, melo kol ha-aretz k'vodo. Az b'kol ra-ash gadol adir v'chazak mash-mi-im kol, mit-nas-im l'umat seraphim, l'umatam baruch yo-mayru.*

"'**Holy,** holy, holy, God of hosts, the whole world is filled with His glory.' Then with a huge, strong, and great sound, a voice is heard, rising facing the seraphim-angels — and opposite them, blessings are said."

*Congregation, repeated by cantor:*

**בָּרוּךְ** כְּבוֹד יְיָ מִמְּקוֹמוֹ. מִמְּקוֹמְךָ מַלְכֵּנוּ תוֹפִיעַ, וְתִמְלֹךְ עָלֵינוּ, כִּי מְחַכִּים אֲנַחְנוּ לָךְ. מָתַי תִּמְלֹךְ בְּצִיּוֹן, בְּקָרוֹב בְּיָמֵינוּ, לְעוֹלָם וָעֶד תִּשְׁכּוֹן. תִּתְגַּדַּל וְתִתְקַדַּשׁ בְּתוֹךְ יְרוּשָׁלַיִם עִירְךָ, לְדוֹר וָדוֹר וּלְנֵצַח נְצָחִים. וְעֵינֵינוּ תִרְאֶינָה מַלְכוּתֶךָ, כַּדָּבָר הָאָמוּר בְּשִׁירֵי עֻזֶּךָ, עַל יְדֵי דָוִד מְשִׁיחַ צִדְקֶךָ:

*Shabbat*

***Baruch*** *k'vod Adonoi mim-komo. Mim-komcha malkaynu tofi-ah, v'tim-loch alaynu ki m'chakim anachnu lach. Matai timloch b'tziyon b'karov b'yamaynu, l'olam va-ed tishkon. Tit-gadel v'tit-kadesh b'toch Yerushalayim ircha, l'dor va-dor u-l'netzach n'tzachim. V'aynaynu tir-ena mal-chu-techa, kadavar ha-amur b'shiray u-zecha, al y'day David mashiach tzid-kecha.*

**"'Blessed** is the glory of God from His place.' From Your place, our King, appear, and reign over us, for we are waiting for You! When will You rule over us in Zion, soon, and in our days, forever and ever may You dwell there? May You be made great and sanctified in the midst of Jerusalem Your city, from one generation to the next and for all eternity! May our eyes see Your kingship, as it is said in Your songs of strength, via King David, Your righteous anointed one."

*Congregation, repeated by cantor:*

יִמְלֹךְ יְיָ לְעוֹלָם, אֱלֹהַיִךְ צִיּוֹן, לְדֹר וָדֹר, הַלְלוּיָהּ.

***Yimloch*** *Adonoi l'olam, Elohai-yich tziyon l'dor va-dor, halleluyah!*

**"May** God, Your God, Zion, reign from one generation to the next, praise God!"

*Cantor:*

לְדוֹר וָדוֹר נַגִּיד גָּדְלֶךָ, וּלְנֵצַח נְצָחִים קְדֻשָּׁתְךָ נַקְדִּישׁ, וְשִׁבְחֲךָ, אֱלֹהֵינוּ, מִפִּינוּ לֹא יָמוּשׁ לְעוֹלָם וָעֶד, כִּי אֵל מֶלֶךְ גָּדוֹל וְקָדוֹשׁ אָתָּה. בָּרוּךְ אַתָּה יְיָ, הָאֵל הַקָּדוֹשׁ.

***L'dor*** *va-dor nagid gad-lecha u-l'netzach n'tzachim k'dushat-cha nakdish, v'shiv-chacha Elohaynu mi-pinu lo yamush l'olam va-ed, ki El melech gadol v'kadosh Ata. Baruch Ata Adonoi, ha-el ha-kadosh.*

***From*** one generation to the next we will relate Your greatness, and for all eternity we will sanctify Your holiness, and your praises, God, will not depart from our mouths forever and ever, for You are our great and holy God and King. Blessed are You, God, God and King.

## HOLINESS OF THE DAY

*The following segment is unique to Shabbat prayers and discusses the meaning of the day.*

יִשְׂמַח מֹשֶׁה בְּמַתְּנַת חֶלְקוֹ, כִּי עֶבֶד נֶאֱמָן קָרָאתָ לּוֹ. כְּלִיל תִּפְאֶרֶת בְּרֹאשׁוֹ נָתַתָּ (לוֹ), בְּעָמְדוֹ לְפָנֶיךָ עַל הַר סִינַי. וּשְׁנֵי לוּחוֹת אֲבָנִים הוֹרִיד בְּיָדוֹ, וְכָתוּב בָּהֶם שְׁמִירַת שַׁבָּת, וְכֵן כָּתוּב בְּתוֹרָתֶךָ:

וְשָׁמְרוּ בְנֵי יִשְׂרָאֵל אֶת הַשַּׁבָּת, לַעֲשׂוֹת אֶת הַשַּׁבָּת לְדֹרֹתָם בְּרִית עוֹלָם. בֵּינִי וּבֵין בְּנֵי יִשְׂרָאֵל אוֹת הִיא לְעֹלָם, כִּי שֵׁשֶׁת יָמִים עָשָׂה יְיָ אֶת הַשָּׁמַיִם וְאֶת הָאָרֶץ, וּבַיּוֹם הַשְּׁבִיעִי שָׁבַת וַיִּנָּפַשׁ.

***Yismach*** *Moshe b'matnat chelko, ki eved ne-eman karata lo. K'lil tiferet b'rosho natata lo, b'amdo l'fanecha al Har Sinai. U-shnay luchot avanim horid b'yado v'katuv bahem shmirat Shabbat, v'ken katuv b'Torah-techa: "V'shamru v'nai Yisrael et ha-Shabbat, la-asot et ha-Shabbat l'dorotam brit olam, bay-ni*

*Shabbat* 139

u-vayn bnai Yisrael ot hee l'olam ki shay-shet yamim asa Adonoi et ha-shamayim v'et ha-aretz u-vayom ha-shvi-i shavat va-yinafash."

**Moses** rejoiced in the gift of his portion, for he was, as You called him, a loyal servant. You gifted him with a crown of glory as he stood before You at Mount Sinai, and he brought down two tablets of stone in his hand, and in them was written about observing the Sabbath, and this is what's written in Your Torah: "The children of Israel observed the Sabbath, to do Sabbath for generations as an eternal sign between Me and between the children of Israel — it is a sign forever that in six days God created the heavens and earth, and on the seventh day He rested and was refreshed."

וְלֹא נְתַתּוֹ יְיָ אֱלֹהֵינוּ לְגוֹיֵי הָאֲרָצוֹת, וְלֹא הִנְחַלְתּוֹ מַלְכֵּנוּ לְעוֹבְדֵי פְסִילִים, וְגַם בִּמְנוּחָתוֹ לֹא יִשְׁכְּנוּ עֲרֵלִים. כִּי לְיִשְׂרָאֵל עַמְּךָ נְתַתּוֹ בְּאַהֲבָה, לְזֶרַע יַעֲקֹב אֲשֶׁר בָּם בָּחָרְתָּ. עַם מְקַדְּשֵׁי שְׁבִיעִי, כֻּלָּם יִשְׂבְּעוּ וְיִתְעַנְּגוּ מִטּוּבֶךָ, וּבַשְּׁבִיעִי רָצִיתָ בּוֹ וְקִדַּשְׁתּוֹ, חֶמְדַּת יָמִים אוֹתוֹ קָרָאתָ, זֵכֶר לְמַעֲשֵׂה בְרֵאשִׁית.

**V'lo** n'tato Adonoi Elohaynu l'goyay ha-aratzot, v'lo hinchal-to mal-kaynu l'ovday f'silim, v'gam bim-nuchato lo yish-k'nu araylim. Ki l'Yisrael amcha n'tato b'ahava l'zera Yaakov asher bam bacharta. Am mekad-shay sh'vi-i kulam yis-b'u v'yit-angu mi-tuvecha, u-va-shvi-i ratzita bo v'kidashto chemdat yamim oto karata zecher l'ma-asay v'ray-sheet.

**And** You did not give it [Shabbat], God, our God, to the nations of the earth, and didn't bequeath it, our King, to those who worship idols, and the uncircumcised will not enjoy its rest, for You gave it to the Jewish people with love, to the children of Jacob whom You have chosen. The nation who sanctifies the seventh day, all will be satisfied and derive enjoyment from Your goodness, and You desired the seventh day and made it holy. "Most desired of days" You called it, as a remembrance of the works of creation.

אֱלֹהֵינוּ וֵאלֹהֵי אֲבוֹתֵינוּ, רְצֵה בִמְנוּחָתֵנוּ, קַדְּשֵׁנוּ בְּמִצְוֹתֶיךָ, וְתֵן חֶלְקֵנוּ בְּתוֹרָתֶךָ, שַׂבְּעֵנוּ מִטּוּבֶךָ, וְשַׂמְּחֵנוּ בִּישׁוּעָתֶךָ, וְטַהֵר לִבֵּנוּ לְעָבְדְּךָ בֶּאֱמֶת, וְהַנְחִילֵנוּ יְיָ אֱלֹהֵינוּ בְּאַהֲבָה וּבְרָצוֹן שַׁבַּת קָדְשֶׁךָ, וְיָנוּחוּ בוֹ יִשְׂרָאֵל מְקַדְּשֵׁי שְׁמֶךָ. בָּרוּךְ אַתָּה יְיָ, מְקַדֵּשׁ הַשַּׁבָּת.

**Elohaynu** vay-lohay avotay-nu, r'tzay bim-nucha-taynu, kad-shaynu b'mitz-votecha, v'ten chel-kaynu b'Torah-techa, sabaynu mi-tuvecha v'samchaynu bi-shu-atecha, v'taher libaynu l'avd'cha b'emet. V'hanchi-laynu Adonoi Elohaynu b'ahava u-v'ratzon Shabbat kadshecha v'ya-nuchu vo Yisrael mekad-shay sh'mecha. Baruch Ata Adonoi, mekadesh ha-Shabbat.

**Our** God and the God of our ancestors, be satisfied with our rest. Make us holy with Your commandments, and allow us to have a part in Your Torah. Satisfy us with Your goodness and bring us happiness with Your salvation. Purify our hearts to serve You in truth. Give us as a portion, God, our God, with love and goodwill,

*Shabbat*

Your holy Sabbath, and may the Jewish people, who sanctify Your name, rest on it. Blessed are You, God, Who sanctifies the Sabbath.

God, I recognize what a huge gift Shabbat is. I know my relationship to Shabbat isn't all it should be. I should clue in more, unplug more, pay more attention to what really counts. But even in my imperfect state, I recognize how lucky we are. You gifted Shabbat to us with love — because You love us, and You wanted us to have the gift of rest, of serenity, of getting off the hamster wheel once a week to remember why we were on it in the first place (or why we should get off for good).

God, I understand that Shabbat is a special sign between You and us, the Jewish people. You Yourself stopped creating after six days. You showed us that epic relationship between work and rest; between getting out there and controlling the world, and stopping and sitting back and realizing that the world won't stop turning if we withdraw for a bit.

---

> YOU SHOWED US THAT EPIC RELATIONSHIP BETWEEN WORK AND REST; BETWEEN GETTING OUT THERE AND CONTROLLING THE WORLD, AND STOPPING AND SITTING BACK AND REALIZING THAT THE WORLD WON'T STOP TURNING IF WE WITHDRAW FOR A BIT.

---

God, You intended for Shabbat to be delicious, delightful, and joyous. I'm going to try to bring more of that into my life. So, on that note, God — Shabbat Shalom to You, to me, and to the entire Jewish people. Thank You, God, for the gift of rest.

## ACCEPT OUR PRAYERS

**רְצֵה**, יְיָ אֱלֹהֵינוּ, בְּעַמְּךָ יִשְׂרָאֵל וּבִתְפִלָּתָם, וְהָשֵׁב אֶת הָעֲבוֹדָה לִדְבִיר בֵּיתֶךָ, וְאִשֵּׁי יִשְׂרָאֵל, וּתְפִלָּתָם בְּאַהֲבָה תְקַבֵּל בְּרָצוֹן, וּתְהִי לְרָצוֹן תָּמִיד עֲבוֹדַת יִשְׂרָאֵל עַמֶּךָ

וְתֶחֱזֶינָה עֵינֵינוּ בְּשׁוּבְךָ לְצִיּוֹן בְּרַחֲמִים. בָּרוּךְ אַתָּה יְיָ, הַמַּחֲזִיר שְׁכִינָתוֹ לְצִיּוֹן.

**R'tzay** *Adonoi Elohaynu b'amcha Yisrael u-vi-tefilatam, v'hashev et ha-avodah li-dvir bay-techa. V'ishay Yisrael u-tefilatam, b'ahava tekabel b'ratzon, u-tehi l'ratzon tamid avodat Yisrael amecha. V'techezena aynaynu b'shuvcha l'tziyon b'rachamim. Baruch Ata Adonoi, ha-machazir shechi-nato l'tziyon.*

**God,** our God, desire Your nation Israel, and their prayers, and restore the temple service to the sanctuary of Your home. Accept with love and willingness the offerings and prayers of the Jewish people, and may the service of Your nation Israel always be favorable to You. May our eyes see Your return to Zion with compassion. Blessed are You, God, Who restores His holy presence to Zion.

God, back in Temple times, we could talk to You with our belongings. We would offer you our possessions, and see that You'd accepted them. Now, life is far more ambiguous. I stand here and offer You my innermost yearnings, and just pray that they are accepted. As I come toward the end of the Amidah, I ask: please accept my words in the manner that they're offered — in earnestness, sincerity, and honesty. And one day, maybe I'll be able to visit the Temple again, and see that miracle of acceptance with my own eyes.

## GRATITUDE

*Bow at the beginning and end of this prayer.*

מוֹדִים אֲנַחְנוּ לָךְ, שָׁאַתָּה הוּא, יְיָ אֱלֹהֵינוּ וֵאלֹהֵי אֲבוֹתֵינוּ, לְעוֹלָם וָעֶד, צוּר חַיֵּינוּ, מָגֵן יִשְׁעֵנוּ, אַתָּה הוּא לְדוֹר וָדוֹר, נוֹדֶה

*Shabbat* 143

לְךָ וּנְסַפֵּר תְּהִלָּתֶךָ, עַל חַיֵּינוּ הַמְּסוּרִים בְּיָדֶךָ, וְעַל נִשְׁמוֹתֵינוּ הַפְּקוּדוֹת לָךְ, וְעַל נִסֶּיךָ שֶׁבְּכָל יוֹם עִמָּנוּ, וְעַל נִפְלְאוֹתֶיךָ וְטוֹבוֹתֶיךָ שֶׁבְּכָל עֵת, עֶרֶב וָבֹקֶר וְצָהֳרָיִם, הַטּוֹב, כִּי לֹא כָלוּ רַחֲמֶיךָ, וְהַמְרַחֵם, כִּי לֹא תַמּוּ חֲסָדֶיךָ, מֵעוֹלָם קִוִּינוּ לָךְ.

**וְעַל** כֻּלָּם יִתְבָּרַךְ וְיִתְרוֹמַם שִׁמְךָ מַלְכֵּנוּ תָּמִיד לְעוֹלָם וָעֶד. וְכֹל הַחַיִּים יוֹדוּךָ סֶּלָה, וִיהַלְלוּ אֶת שִׁמְךָ בֶּאֱמֶת, הָאֵל יְשׁוּעָתֵנוּ וְעֶזְרָתֵנוּ סֶלָה. בָּרוּךְ אַתָּה יְיָ, הַטּוֹב שִׁמְךָ וּלְךָ נָאֶה לְהוֹדוֹת.

**Modim** anachnu lach, she-Ata hu Adonoi Elohaynu vay-lohay avotaynu, l'olam va-ed. Tzur chai-aynu, magen yish-aynu Ata hu l'dor va-dor. Nodeh l'cha u-nesaper tehilatecha al chai-aynu ha-mesurim b'yadecha v'al nish-motaynu ha-pedudot lach, v'al nisecha she-b'chol yom imanu, v'al nifle-otecha v'tovotecha, she-b'chol ayt, erev va-voker v'tzaharayim. Ha-tov ki lo chalu rachamecha, v'ha-merachem ki lo tamu chasadecha, may-olam kivinu lach.

**V'al** kulam yit-barach v'yit-romam v'yit-nasay shimcha malkaynu tamid l'olam va-ed. V'chol ha-chaim yoducha selah, vi-hallelu et shimcha be-emet, ha-El y'shu-ataynu v'ezrataynu selah. Baruch Ata Adonoi, ha-tov shimcha u-l'cha na-eh l'hodot.

**We** give thanks before You, that You are God, our God, and the God of our ancestors, forever. You are the rock of our lives, the shield of our salvation, from generation to generation. We will thank You, and tell the story of Your praise, about our lives, which are entrusted to Your *hands, and about our souls, which are safeguarded with You, and about Your miracles which are with us every day, and about Your wonders and good deeds, that are with us always — evening, morning, and afternoon. You are good, because Your compassion never ends, and You are compassionate, because Your kindnesses never cease. May we always hope to You.*

**And** *for all of these, may Your name be blessed, exalted, elevated, our God, always and forever. And may all the living thank You, forever, and praise Your name in truth, oh, God, our salvation and our helper, forever. Blessed are You, God, Whose name is good, and to You it is fitting to thank.*

God, I sincerely want to say thank You. For being our God. For being our Rock. For our lives, that are dependent on You. For our souls, that are a spark of You. For Your small miracles that are with us every day. For the good things You do for us every moment of every day. Your compassion never runs out! Your kindnesses never stop! "Thank you" almost seems pathetic. But it's the best I've got, God. For all these, God, I hope humans always recognize Your greatness. And I, for one, will do my share and resolve to be more grateful.

## PEACE

שִׂים שָׁלוֹם טוֹבָה וּבְרָכָה, חֵן וָחֶסֶד וְרַחֲמִים, עָלֵינוּ וְעַל כָּל יִשְׂרָאֵל עַמֶּךָ. בָּרְכֵנוּ, אָבִינוּ, כֻּלָּנוּ כְּאֶחָד בְּאוֹר פָּנֶיךָ, כִּי בְאוֹר פָּנֶיךָ נָתַתָּ לָּנוּ, יְיָ אֱלֹהֵינוּ, תּוֹרַת חַיִּים וְאַהֲבַת חֶסֶד, וּצְדָקָה וּבְרָכָה וְרַחֲמִים וְחַיִּים וְשָׁלוֹם, וְטוֹב בְּעֵינֶיךָ לְבָרֵךְ אֶת עַמְּךָ יִשְׂרָאֵל בְּכָל עֵת וּבְכָל שָׁעָה בִּשְׁלוֹמֶךָ.

בָּרוּךְ אַתָּה יְיָ, הַמְבָרֵךְ אֶת עַמּוֹ יִשְׂרָאֵל בַּשָּׁלוֹם.

**Sim** *shalom tova u-vracha chayn va-chesed v'rachamim, alaynu v'al kol Yisrael amecha, barchaynu avinu kulanu k'echad b'or panecha, ki v'or panecha natata lanu Adonoi Elohaynu torat chaim v'ahavat chesed, u-tzedaka u-vracha v'rachamim v'chaim v'shalom v'tov b'aynecha l'varech et amcha Yisrael b'chol ayt u-v'chol sha-ah bi-shlomecha. Baruch Ata Adonoi, ha-mevarech et amo Yisrael ba-shalom.*

**Establish** *peace, goodness, blessing, grace, kindness, and compassion on us and on all of Israel, Your nation. Bless us, our Father, all of us as one, with the light of Your face, for with the light of Your face you've given us — God, our God — a Torah of life, love of kindness, charity, blessing, compassion, life, peace, and goodness. May it be good in Your eyes to bless all of Your nation Israel, at all times and in every moment, with Your peace. Blessed are You, God, Who blesses His nation Israel with peace.*

God, please help our world to be more peaceful. I pray not just for peace, but for lots of other things that go along with it: goodness, blessing, life, mutual respect, kindness, compassion. Bless us with Your special, peaceful light — that "holiness" that I mentioned earlier. It was that light with which You gifted us the Torah. It hurts me so much that Jewish people misunderstand each other so badly and that there is so much horrible infighting. I imagine it must pain You too, God. Please: bless Your people Israel, always, with peace.

## CONCLUSION

אֱלֹהַי, נְצוֹר לְשׁוֹנִי מֵרָע, וּשְׂפָתַי מִדַּבֵּר מִרְמָה, וְלִמְקַלְלַי נַפְשִׁי תִדֹּם, וְנַפְשִׁי כֶּעָפָר לַכֹּל תִּהְיֶה. פְּתַח לִבִּי בְּתוֹרָתֶךָ,

וּבְמִצְוֹתֶיךָ תִּרְדּוֹף נַפְשִׁי. וְכָל הַחוֹשְׁבִים עָלַי רָעָה, מְהֵרָה הָפֵר עֲצָתָם וְקַלְקֵל מַחֲשַׁבְתָּם. עֲשֵׂה לְמַעַן שְׁמֶךָ, עֲשֵׂה לְמַעַן יְמִינֶךָ, עֲשֵׂה לְמַעַן קְדֻשָּׁתֶךָ, עֲשֵׂה לְמַעַן תּוֹרָתֶךָ. לְמַעַן יֵחָלְצוּן יְדִידֶיךָ, הוֹשִׁיעָה יְמִינְךָ וַעֲנֵנִי. יִהְיוּ לְרָצוֹן אִמְרֵי פִי וְהֶגְיוֹן לִבִּי לְפָנֶיךָ, יְיָ צוּרִי וְגוֹאֲלִי. עֹשֶׂה שָׁלוֹם בִּמְרוֹמָיו, הוּא יַעֲשֶׂה שָׁלוֹם עָלֵינוּ, וְעַל כָּל יִשְׂרָאֵל, וְאִמְרוּ אָמֵן.

**Elohai,** netzor l'shoni mayra u-sefatai mi-daber mirma. V'lim-ka-lelai nafshi tidom, v'nafshi ke-afar lakol ti-hiyeh. P'tach libi b'Torah-techa u-v'mitzvotecha tirdof nafshi, v'chol ha-choshvim alai ra-ah m'hayra ha-fayr atzatam v'kalkel macha-shavtam. Asay l'ma-an sh'mecha, asay l'ma-an y'minecha, asay l'ma-an k'dusha-techa, asay l'ma-an Torah-techa. L'ma-an yay-chal-tzun y'didecha, ho-shiya yemincha va-anayni. Yi-hiyu l'ratzon imray fi, v'heg-yon libi l'fanecha, Adonoi tzuri v'go-ali.

**My** God. Restrain my tongue from bad, and my lips from speaking deceitfully. May my soul be silent when others curse me, and may my essence be like dust to all. Open my heart in Your Torah and may my soul pursue Your mitzvot. May all those who wish evil for me have their plots quickly nullified and their plans ruined. Do it for Your name, do it for Your right hand, do it for Your holiness, do it for Your Torah. Save Your right hand and answer me so that Your dear ones may rest. May the words of my mouth and the thoughts of my heart be favorable before You, God, my Rock and Redeemer.

*Take three steps backward to symbolize moving out of the immediate company of God.*

*Shabbat*

*Bow left and say: Oseh shalom bi-mromav*

*He Who makes peace in the heavens*

*Bow right and say: Hu ya-aseh shalom alaynu*

*may He make peace upon us*

*Bow forward and say: V'al kol Yisrael*

*and on all Israel.*

*Straighten up and say: V'imru amen.*

*And we say, Amen.*

יְהִי רָצוֹן מִלְּפָנֶיךָ, יְיָ אֱלֹהֵינוּ וֵאלֹהֵי אֲבוֹתֵינוּ, שֶׁיִּבָּנֶה בֵּית הַמִּקְדָּשׁ בִּמְהֵרָה בְיָמֵינוּ, וְתֵן חֶלְקֵנוּ בְּתוֹרָתֶךָ, וְשָׁם נַעֲבָדְךָ בְּיִרְאָה כִּימֵי עוֹלָם וּכְשָׁנִים קַדְמוֹנִיּוֹת. וְעָרְבָה לַייָ מִנְחַת יְהוּדָה וִירוּשָׁלָיִם, כִּימֵי עוֹלָם וּכְשָׁנִים קַדְמוֹנִיּוֹת.

**Y'hi** ratzon mil-fanecha, Adonoi Elohaynu vaylohay avotaynu, she-yibaneh bayt ha-mikdash bim'hayra v'yamaynu, v'tayn chelkaynu b'Torah-tehcha, v'sham na-avadcha b'yira kimay olam u-ch'shanim kadmoniyot. V'arva la-Adonoi minchat Yehuda vi-Yerushalayim ki-may olam u-ch'shanim kadmoniyot.

**May** it be Your will, God, our God, and the God of our ancestors, that You build the Holy Temple quickly and in our days, and give us our place in Your Torah. There, may we worship You in reverence, like in the days of old and in bygone years. And may the offerings of Judah and Jerusalem be favorable before God like in the days of old and in bygone years.

*Take three steps forward. This concludes the Amidah service.*

# Havdallah

*Havdallah is a very moving tradition. It is a prayer recited after nightfall on Saturday night to formally mark the closure of Shabbat. Even if a Jew does not celebrate or observe Shabbat fully, he still can fulfill the mitzvah of Havdallah. The ceremony is conducted with the following supplies: a multi-wicked candle, an overflowing cup of wine or grape juice, and spices to smell such as cloves or cinnamon. The multi-wicked candle represents that we begin Shabbat with two separate flames, but by the time Shabbat ends, all its lessons and impacts are intertwined within us and fully integrated. The overflowing cup signifies our prayerful hope that the effects of Shabbat overflow into our mundane workweek. And the spices are to inhale the "aroma" of Shabbat, to stay with us when it's gone. When the cup is full and the candle lit, the leader, or individual, recites the prayer.*

---

> THE OVERFLOWING CUP SIGNIFIES OUR PRAYERFUL HOPE THAT THE EFFECTS OF SHABBAT OVERFLOW INTO OUR MUNDANE WORKWEEK.

---

הִנֵּה אֵל יְשׁוּעָתִי, אֶבְטַח וְלֹא אֶפְחָד, כִּי עָזִּי וְזִמְרָת יָהּ יְיָ, וַיְהִי לִי לִישׁוּעָה. וּשְׁאַבְתֶּם מַיִם בְּשָׂשׂוֹן, מִמַּעַיְנֵי הַיְשׁוּעָה. לַייָ הַיְשׁוּעָה, עַל עַמְּךָ בִרְכָתֶךָ סֶּלָה. יְיָ צְבָאוֹת עִמָּנוּ, מִשְׂגָּב לָנוּ אֱלֹהֵי יַעֲקֹב סֶלָה. יְיָ צְבָאוֹת, אַשְׁרֵי אָדָם בֹּטֵחַ בָּךְ. יְיָ הוֹשִׁיעָה, הַמֶּלֶךְ יַעֲנֵנוּ בְיוֹם קָרְאֵנוּ.

*Introductory verses:*

**Hi-nay** El y'shu-ati evtach v'lo efchad, ki azi v'zimrat Yah Adonoi vai-y'hi li li-shu-ah. U-sh'av-tem mayim b'sason mi-mai-nay ha-y'shu-ah. La-Adonoi ha-y'shu-ah al amcha bir-cha-techa selah. Adonoi tz'va-ot imanu misgav lanu Elohay Yaakov selah. Adonoi tz'va-ot ash-ray adam bo-tayach bach. Adonoi ho-shi-a ha-melech ya-a-nay-nu b'yom kar-ay-nu.

**Behold,** *God of my salvation, I will trust and not fear, for God is my strength and praise, and was a salvation for me. You will draw waters with joy from the wellsprings of salvation. Salvation is God's; Your blessings are on Your nation, forever! God of hosts is with us, as a strength for us, is the God of Jacob, forever! God of hosts, fortunate is he who trusts in You! God, save! May the King answer us on the day that we call Him.*

*All recite:*

לַיְּהוּדִים הָיְתָה אוֹרָה וְשִׂמְחָה וְשָׂשׂוֹן וִיקָר. כֵּן תִּהְיֶה לָּנוּ.

**La-ye-hudim** hay-ta ora v'simcha v'sason vi-kar, ken ti-hi-yeh lanu.

**The** Jews had light, happiness, joy, and honor. So may it be for us.

*Leader repeats:*

לַיְּהוּדִים הָיְתָה אוֹרָה וְשִׂמְחָה וְשָׂשׂוֹן וִיקָר. כֵּן תִּהְיֶה לָּנוּ.

**La-ye-hudim** hay-ta ora v'simcha v'sason vi-kar, ken ti-hi-yeh lanu.

**The** Jews had light, happiness, joy, and honor. So may it be for us.

*Leader continues:*

כּוֹס יְשׁוּעוֹת אֶשָּׂא, וּבְשֵׁם יְיָ אֶקְרָא.

**Kos** y'shu-ot esa u-v'shem Adonoi ekra.

**I will** lift the cup of salvation, and call in the name of God.

*Lift the cup of wine and say:*

בָּרוּךְ אַתָּה יְיָ, אֱלֹהֵינוּ מֶלֶךְ הָעוֹלָם, בּוֹרֵא פְּרִי הַגָּפֶן.

**Baruch** Ata Adonoi, Elohaynu melech ha-olam, boray pri ha-gafen.

**Blessed** are You, God, our God, King of the universe, Who created the fruit of the vine.

*All attending say: Amen.*

*Hold the spices and say:*

בָּרוּךְ אַתָּה יְיָ, אֱלֹהֵינוּ מֶלֶךְ הָעוֹלָם, בּוֹרֵא מִינֵי בְשָׂמִים.

**Baruch** Ata Adonoi, Elohaynu melech ha-olam, boray mi-nay v'samim.

**Blessed** are You, God, our God, King of the universe, Who created species of spices.

*All attending say: Amen. Everyone smells the spices.*

*Hold the candle and say:*

בָּרוּךְ אַתָּה יְיָ, אֱלֹהֵינוּ מֶלֶךְ הָעוֹלָם, בּוֹרֵא מְאוֹרֵי הָאֵשׁ.

**Baruch** Ata Adonoi, Elohaynu melech ha-olam, boray m'oray ha-esh.

**Blessed** are You, God, our God, King of the universe, Who created the lights of fire.

*Shabbat*

*All attending say: Amen.*

*There is a kabbalistic custom to see the candlelight reflected in one's fingernails.*

*Leader continues:*

בָּרוּךְ אַתָּה יְיָ, אֱלֹהֵינוּ מֶלֶךְ הָעוֹלָם, הַמַּבְדִיל בֵּין קֹדֶשׁ לְחוֹל, בֵּין אוֹר לְחֹשֶׁךְ, בֵּין יִשְׂרָאֵל לָעַמִּים, בֵּין יוֹם הַשְּׁבִיעִי לְשֵׁשֶׁת יְמֵי הַמַּעֲשֶׂה. בָּרוּךְ אַתָּה יְיָ, הַמַּבְדִיל בֵּין קֹדֶשׁ לְחוֹל.

**Baruch** Ata Adonoi, Elohaynu melech ha-olam, ha-mavdil bayn kodesh l'chol, bayn or l'choshech, bayn Yisrael la-amim, bayn yom ha-shvi-i l'shay-shet y'may ha-ma-seh, baruch Ata Adonoi, ha-mavdil bayn kodesh l'chol.

**Blessed** are You, God, our God, King of the universe, Who has distinguished between holy and mundane; between light and dark; between Israel and the nations; between the seventh day and the six days of creation. Blessed are You, God, Who has distinguished between the holy and the mundane.

*Part Four:*

# VARIOUS PRAYERS

The essential mitzvah of prayer is to talk to God in our own words, spontaneously. Since most of us wouldn't do this frequently enough, scripts have been written to help us articulate our needs. Historically, an important part of prayer has been "techinot" (appeals) — written throughout the ages — for various needs one might encounter in daily living. Below appear abridged forms of these techinot in Hebrew and English, as well as some originals in English only.

# FAMILY

## To Find a Soulmate

**Yehi** ratzon mil-fanecha, Adonoi Elo-hai vay-lohay avotai, she-tamtzi li birachamecha ha-rabim u-va-chasadecha ha-gedolim et zivugi ha-ra-uy li bizmano. Vioto ish she-tamtzi li lizivugi y'hay ish tov, ish na-eh bima-asav, baal maasim tovim, baal chen, ish maskil vi-ray Elohim, rodef tzedakah vigomel tov. Vilo y'hay bo shemetz u-pesul, u-mum u-pegam, vilo y'hay ka-asan viragzan, rak ba-al anavah u-n'michut ruach, bari u-ba-al koach, vial ye-akev achzariyut ha-briyot vi-sonim u-mach-sh'vo-tayhem vitach-bu-lo-tayhem liakev et ben zugi ha-muchan li. Yi-hi-yu liratzon imray fi vihegyon libi lifanecha, Adonoi tzuri vigoali.

**May** it be Your will, God, my God, and the God of my ancestors, that You find for me, in Your abundant compassion and great kindness, the soulmate that is just right for me, at the right time. And this man that You find for me as a soulmate should be a good man, a man who is

Various Prayers 155

*pleasant in his deeds, who does good things, who has grace, wisdom, and reverence for God; who pursues tzedakah and does acts of kindness for others. May there not be found in him deficiencies and ugliness; defects and faults. May he not have a temper or angry nature; rather, may he be humble and self-effacing; healthy and strong. May the cruelty of others and of haters, of their plots and plans, not prevent me from meeting my intended soulmate. May the words of my mouth and the thoughts of my heart find favor before You, God, my Rock and Redeemer.*

God, I've been looking for my *basherte*, and I need Your help. You have chosen a soulmate for me, someone who will complete me and help me along in this journey called life. I am looking for someone with whom to create a life, a family, a future — someone to love and be loved by; someone with whom to share life's ups and downs; someone with whom to build our Jewish legacy. God, help me to find the right person who will have refined character and spirituality; who won't be afraid to tell me, in a kind way, where I need to improve; who won't forget to tell me how wonderful I am; who can laugh with me and cry with me and help me perfect my soul and reach my potential. May he be kind, healthy, spiritual, loving, and strong. Please God, help me to meet my soulmate quickly and easily, with clarity and joy.

## On One's Wedding Day

**God,** today is one of the most important days of my life. I ask You that You allow my husband and me to be blessed with holiness in our marriage and that Your presence grace our lives. Give us purity of soul, that neither of us have eyes for anyone else but each other. May it be in my eyes as though there were no other man in the world as good, as handsome, and as charming, and may I be in the eyes of my husband as if there were no other woman in the world as beautiful, as charming, and as fitting for him. May his thoughts always be about me, and about no one else, as it says in Genesis, "Therefore shall a man leave his father and his mother and cleave to his wife."

May our marriage prosper with love, peace, and friendship; may it be in accordance with the teachings of Moses and Judaism; may it be endowed with reverence for God; may it produce wholesome and righteous children. May it be a marriage of blessing and in which my husband will be happy with me and I with him more than anything else in the world.

I am hereby prepared to live a Jewish life and raise a Jewish family and to enter the chuppah with my fiancée. Please, at this holy moment, forgive us for all our sins and mistakes and let us start out our marriage with a pure and clean slate upon which to build, and shower upon us goodness, blessing, love, and holiness all the days of our lives.

## Mikveh Prayer

The mitzvah for married women to visit the mikveh is one of their three unique mitzvot, along with lighting Shabbat candles and separating the challah. It is a special time of holiness and prayer.

Various Prayers

## BEFORE IMMERSING:

**Master** of the universe, You have brought sanctity into the world, and have sanctified the Jewish people. You've commanded us to be holy and to enter the waters of the mikveh in order to purify and sanctify our bodies. God, please may my mitzvah of immersing in the mikveh waters be pleasing before You, and may my mitzvah be accepted by You. Just as so many Jewish women before me immersed in the mikveh, even during very difficult times in our history, and showed so much self-sacrifice and determination for this mitzvah, so too am I linking myself in that chain of strong, committed Jewish women fulfilling this mitzvah. Hear my prayer, bless me and my husband with grace and joy and fulfill all my prayers for a beautiful marriage and wonderful children. May Your holy presence hover over us; imbue within us a spirit of purity; may we always be happy with one another; shower upon us all the blessings in the world, that we may live long, happy lives in which to do Your mitzvot. Amen.

## JUST BEFORE ENTERING MIKVEH:

בָּרוּךְ אַתָּה יְיָ אֱלֹהֵינוּ מֶלֶךְ הָעוֹלָם, אֲשֶׁר קִדְּשָׁנוּ בְּמִצְוֹתָיו וְצִוָּנוּ עַל הַטְּבִילָה.

**Baruch** Ata Adonoi, Elohaynu melech ha-olam, asher kid-shanu b'mitz-votav v'tzivanu, al ha-tevilah.

**Blessed** are You, God, our God, King of the universe, Who has sanctified us with His commandments and has commanded us regarding immersion.

## A Woman's Prayer for Her Husband and for Their Marriage

**Y'hi** ratzon mil-fanecha, Adonoi Elohai vay-lohay avotai, she-tish-mor v'tin-tzor v'tin-tor tamid et ba-ali mi-kol nezek u-mi-kol ra u-mi-kol choli. V'ti-ten lo chaim tovim, chaim aruchim, chaim shel osher v'kavod. V'ti-ta bay-naynu tamid ahava v'achva shalom v'rayut. V'tikba ahavati v'lev ba-ali she-lo yachshov b'shum isha ba-olam zulati, v'ti-ta b'li-baynu ahavatcha v'yiratcha, la-asot retzon-cha u-l'avdecha b'levav shalem k'yehudim keshay-rim, v'la-asot tzedaka va-chesed im amcha Yisrael, u-t'varech et ba-ali bracha she-layma b'rov oz v'shalom, ka-davar she-ne-emar: Y'va-rech'cha Adonoi v'yish-m'recha, ya-er Adonoi panav ay-lecha vi-chuneka, yi-sa Adonoi panav ay-lecha, v'yasem l'cha shalom. V'ne-emar: Adonoi yish-m'rayhu v'chai-yay-hu v'ushar ba-aretz. Amen, ken y'hi ratzon.

Various Prayers

**May** it be Your will, God, my God and the God of my ancestors, that You watch over, protect and keep my husband from any harm, anything bad, and any illness. Gift him with a good and long life of happiness and honor. Please instill between us — always — love, camaraderie, peace, and friendship. Establish in my husband's heart a love for me, that he may not think of any other woman besides me. Instill in our hearts a love and reverence for You, to do Your will and serve You with full hearts like good Jews, and to perform charity and kindness with Your people Israel. Bless my husband with a complete blessing and with much strength and peace, as it says: "May God bless you and keep you. May God shine His face upon you and favor you. May God lift his face toward you and set for you peace." And it is also said: "God will watch over him and keep him alive, and he will be happy on earth." Amen, and may it be so.

## To Become Pregnant

**Y'hi** ratzon mil-fanecha, Adonoi Elohai vay-lohay avotai, she-titayn li zera ratzui v'hagun v'tov v'yafeh, m'tukan u-m'kubal, v'ra-uy lichyot u-l'hitkayem bli shum avon v'ashma. V'tashpia bo nefesh v'ruach u-neshama mi-machtzav tahor. U-t'chonen kol ha-chanotav k'day l'hashlimo u-l'kaymo u-l'ha-amido b'noi u-v'chen u-v'chesed u-v'rachamim, b'kav ha-briyut, b'ometz u-b'tokef u-bi-gevurah. U-terachem alav b'hay-a-soto, b'hit-rakmo ay-varav. V'tatzi-gay-hu al bur-yo b'nafsho u-b'rucho u-v'nishmato, bi-kravav u-v'tziyuro. V'lo ye-hay b'echad may-ay-varav, lo nezek v'lo chisaron, lo nega v'lo choli. V'lo yechsar lo kol tuv kol y'may chayav. V'yivaled b'mazal tov u-b'sha-ah tova u-v'racha v'hatz-lacha. V'yich-yeh chaim tovim va-aruchim u-l'shalom, bayn b'ruch-niyut bain b'gashmiyut b'osher v'chavod bi-chlal amcha Yisrael.

**May** it be Your will, God, my God and the God of my ancestors, that You give me a child who is desirable, good, beautiful, accomplished, accepted, and able to live and survive without any sin or mistake. Imbue this child with a pure soul, and grace it with all the gifts that it may be complete to survive and stand on its own in beauty, grace, kindness, and compassion, health, energy, vigor, and strength. Have compassion on it when You are forming it and when You are fashioning its limbs. Allow it to present with wholeness in its mind, soul and spirit; in its insides and shape. May there not be in even one of its limbs any damage, defect, bruise, or illness. May it never lack for anything good all the days of its life. May it be born in a fortunate time and a good hour, in blessing and success. And may it live a good, long, and peaceful life, in both spiritual ways and material ways; with happiness and honor among Your nation Israel. Imbue this child with a pure soul, and grace it with all the gifts that it may be complete to survive and stand on its own in beauty, grace, kindness, and compassion, health, energy, vigor, and strength.

Various Prayers

## During Pregnancy

**Y'hi** *ratzon mil-fanecha, Adonoi Elohai vay-lohay avotai, she-takel may-alai et tza-ar iburi v'tosif v'titen li koach v'on b'chol y'may ha-ibur, she-lo yutash kochi v'lo koach ha-ubar b'shum davar ba-olam, v'tazil oti mi-piska shel Chava u-mi-kilelat, "Harbeh arbeh itz-vo-naych v'hay-ro-naych, b'etzev tel-di banim." Vi-hi b'ayt lid-ti, ki yim-l'u yamai la-ledet, lo yay-haf-chu alai tzirai. V'yay-tzay ha-valad l'avir ha-olam b'rega katon b'kalut b'li shum hezek li v'lo la-valad. V'yi-hi-yeh nolad b'sha-ah tova u-v'mazal tov l'chaim u-l'shalom u-li-briyut, l'chen u-l'chesed, l'osher v'kavod. Va-ani u-ba-ali ne-gad-layhu la-avodatcha u-l'Torat-cha ha-kedosha, u-l'chaim tovim u-l'shalom, v'osher v'kavod u-menucha. V'lo ni-hi-yeh ani v'lo ha-ubar nizokim lo b'guf v'lo b'ay-varim v'lo b'orkim v'lo b'gidim, v'lo b'or u-basar u-she-ar kol binyan b'nay ha-adam, lo b'toch chalal ha-guf v'lo chutz l'chalal ha-guf, u-t'chazek et kochi v'ruchi v'atzmotai. Ken t'var-chay-ni v'ta-anay-ni u-t'cha-nay-ni v'taarich yamai b'ni-imim, amen.*

**May** it be Your will, God, my God and the God of my ancestors, that You ease from upon me the pain of pregnancy, and continue to give me strength and energy all the days of the pregnancy, that my strength and the strength of the fetus not wane in any way in the world. Save me from the curse of Eve [who was told], "I will greatly increase your pain of pregnancy, and you will birth your children with difficulty." May it be that at the time of birth, when the days of gestation are complete, that my pains not overtake me. May the baby emerge to the world in a quick moment, easily, with no damage — not to me, and not to the baby. May it be born in a good hour and fortunate time, for life, peace, and health; for grace, kindness, happiness, and honor. May my husband and I raise the child to serve You and Your holy Torah, for a good life and peace, happiness, honor, and serenity. May neither me nor the baby be harmed — not in body, limbs, blood vessels, sinews, skin, or any other bodily construction, whether internal or external. Strengthen my energy, spirit, and bones, and bless me, answer me, be gracious to me and lengthen my days in pleasantness, amen.

## Husband's Prayer While Wife Is in Labor

**Y'hi** ratzon mil-fanecha, Adonoi Elohai vay-lohay avotai, she-ta-aseh l'ma-an rachamecha ha-rabim u-terachem al [wife's Hebrew name [bat] her mother's Hebrew name] ha-yoshevet al ha-mishbar tzo-eket b'chava-le-ha. El malay rachamim to-tzi-ah may-afay-la l'orah. U-biz-chut imotaynu ha-kedoshot Sarah, Rivka, Rachel, v'Leah, te-rachem aleha v'tif-k'dena li-vracha. Ki ay-nay-nu l'cha teluyot. U-t'vatel may-aleha

Various Prayers 163

kol gezayrot kashot v'ra-ot v'tatzi-la mi-kol tza-ar.
V'yay-tzay ha-valad l'chaim tovim u-l'shalom u-v'sha-
ah tova u-m'vorechet lanu v'la-valad. Y'hi-yu l'ratzon
imray fi v'heg-yon libi l'fanecha, Adonoi tzuri v'go-ali.

**May** it be Your will, God, my God and the God of my ancestors, that You act according to Your great compassion, and have compassion on [wife's Hebrew name (bat) her mother's Hebrew name] who is in labor, crying from her contractions. God Who is full of mercy, take her from darkness to light. In the merit of our matriarchs, Sarah, Rebecca, Rachel, and Leah, have compassion on her and remember her for blessing. Our eyes are turned to You. Please annul any harsh decrees and save her from any distress. May our baby emerge for good life and peace, and in a good and blessed time, for us and for the baby. May the words of my mouth and the thoughts of my heart be favorable before You, God, our Rock and Redeemer.

## After a Miscarriage or Stillbirth

*composed by Tamar Livingstone*

**Knower** of all Knowings, I turn to You from my state of confusion, pain, and loss. My dreams have been shattered, and my future has ended in an instant, a life of potential never to be lived. Help remove the feelings of shame, and restore my feelings of trust in my body's power to act as a vessel *for bringing goodness and holiness into the world. Reassure me that my loss was not a result of my improper actions, a punishment to me, but rather a necessary part of Your plan for me and for my baby. Assuage my feelings of guilt by helping me see that my experience of this tragedy allows me to be the conduit for Your will. Allow me to feel that I was the only mother this baby needed, and that I mothered him/her exactly the way You wanted, for precisely the amount of time he/she needed a mother. Turn this painful loss of potential into the fulfillment of the greatest potential that You had in mind for the precious soul I harbored inside me.*

*Healer of all Healers, I turn to You from my place of despair, and ask for Your compassion, Your strength, and Your blessing as I mourn the loss of what was taken from me, and try to find my way back into Your loving arms.*

*I turn to You, our Father in Heaven, and pray that You will keep my baby in Your arms, so he/she will be safe, protected, and cherished. Nurture and love him/her, and allow him/her to feel how I love him/her as well. He/she will always be a part of me.*

## Parents' Prayer for Their Children

**Y'hi** *ratzon mil-fanecha, Adonoi Elohaynu vay-lohay avo-tay-nu, she-y'hi-u ba-nay-nu me-irim ba-Torah, v'y'hiyu bri-im b'gufam v'sich-lam, ba-alay midot tovot, oskim ba-Torah lishmah. V'tayn lahem chaim aruchim*

*Various Prayers*    165

*v'tovim, v'y'hiyu m'mula-im ba-Torah, u-v'chochmah u-v'yirat shamayim. V'y'hiyu ahuvim l'mala v'nechmadim l'mata. V'tatzi-laym may-ayin hara u-mi-yetzer hara u-mi-kol mi-nay pur-aniyot. V'y'hiyu lahem chushim briyim la-vodatcha. V'zakaynu b'rachamecha ha-rabim v'et ba-ali she-timalay mispar yamaynu b'tov u-b'ni-imim, v'ahava v'shalom. V'nizkeh l'gadel ba-nay-nu u-be-no-taynu l'Torah u-l'chuppah u-l'ma-asim tovim. V'tazmin la-hem zivugam b'nakel, u-l'hasi-am im zivugam b'may ha-ne-urim b'nachat u-b'revach u-v'simcha. V'yo-lidu ba-nay-nu u-be-no-taynu banim tovim tzadikim zochim u-me-zakim l'chol Yisrael. U-malay kol mishalot levavaynu l'tova bi-vriyut v'hatzlacha v'chol tov.*

**May** it be Your will, God, our God and the God of our ancestors, that our children may light up the world with Torah, and may they be healthy in their body and mind, people of good character, involved in Torah for its own sake. Please give them long and good lives, and may they be filled with Torah, wisdom, and reverence for Heaven. May they have confidence in themselves and take pleasure from good choices. May they be beloved Above and treasured below on earth. Save them from the evil eye and from the evil inclination, and from any kind of punishment. May they have healthy senses to serve You. Give us the merit, in Your great compassion [together with my husband] that we may fill out our days in goodness and pleasantness, with love and peace. May we merit to raise our sons and daughters to Torah, to the chuppah, and to good deeds. Prepare for them their soulmates who are good, kind, and will bring out their potential, that they may build a beautiful Jewish home together. Let us marry them off in their youth, with ease, generosity, and happiness. May they give birth to sons and daughters who are good, righteous, and are a credit to Your people Israel. Fulfill all the wishes of our hearts for the good, in good health, success, and all kinds of goodness.

May we merit to raise our sons and daughters to Torah, to the chuppah, and to good deeds.

## Children's Prayer for Their Parents

**Y'hi** ratzon mil-fanecha, Adonoi Elohaynu vay-lohay avo-tay-nu, she-yi-hiyu avinu v'imaynu v'anachnu bri-im va-chazakim l'avdecha be-emet u-v'simcha, v'tayn b'li-baynu lishmo-a b'kol avinu v'imaynu, v'hoshi-aynu she-nichabed otam tamid ka-asher retzoncha ha-tov imanu. V'na-avod otcha b'emet v'gadlu avinu v'imaynu otanu l'Torah u-l'chuppah u-l'ma-asim tovim, v'y'hiyu mutzlachim bi-vriyut v'kol tuv va-ashirut, li-ten lanu mohar u-matan v'kol tuv b'sever panim yafot. U-malay kol mishalot levavaynu l'tova. Avinu she-ba-shamayim, ho-shi-aynu kol zeh bi-chlal kol Yisrael, v'nizkeh l'hagdil k'vod shimcha ha-gadol u-k'vod Toratcha tamid. Yi-hi-yu l'ratzon imray fi v'hegyon libi l'fanecha, Adonoi tzuri v'goali.

**May** it be Your will, God, our God and the God of our ancestors, that our father, our mother, and we be healthy

Various Prayers

*and strong to serve You with love and joy. Instill in our hearts to listen to the voices of our father and mother, and help us to honor them as You will it. And we will serve You in truth. May our parents merit to raise us to lives of Torah, to the chuppah, and to do good deeds, and may they be successful in health and in every good thing; and in wealth, that they be able to provide for us happily. Fulfill all the wishes of our hearts. Our Father in heaven, help us in all these matters, along with all of Israel, and may we merit to raise the honor of Your great name and the honor of Torah. May the words of my mouth and the thoughts of my heart be favorable before You, God, our Rock and Redeemer.*

## Sending Children Off To School

**Dear God,**

Watch over my children. Guide them through the day and keep them safe and protected. May this year be one of learning, of maturity, and of self-development. Help them to learn and grow. May they have friends who appreciate them, teachers who see the good in them, and experiences that will help them become wonderful people. God, may their influences be positive, such that their sweet and innocent and trusting souls be brought to their highest potential. May their academic, emotional, and spiritual selves be developed and nurtured. May their minds be *stretched but not taxed. May their emotions be pulled but not too hard. May their friendships be enriching and not too painful. Above all, God, may they be kind to others and to themselves. May they ask for help when they need it and learn that often they do not need it. Watch over them and bless them in their comings and goings. Amen.*

## For Raising Special Needs Children

**Dear God,**

*You have given me a child* **[insert Hebrew name ben/bat Hebrew name]** *with special needs, and You have entrusted him/her in my care because You trust me with the love and care of this child. Help me to have the patience and wisdom to meet his/her needs. Guide me to the information that will be helpful and not confusing. Lead me to doctors, therapists, and specialists who are the right messengers to partner with us in helping him/her reach his/her potential. Imbue my family and friends with wisdom to support me in the ways I need, and help me to understand when they say and do things that are upsetting or hurtful. [Allow me to meet the needs of my other children in our unique situation. Send special protection for my marriage, that my spouse and I be able to find the tools to nurture our marriage in the difficult times. Help us to find solutions when we don't see eye to eye in the matter of this special child. Help us to remember that our marriage can't* come last. Help us to support each other and find the humor in life.] Protect me from shame, fear, guilt, and overwhelm. Gift me instead with love, pride, confidence, and joy. Let the light of this child illuminate our home and our lives and remind us that every one of us is on a journey with different strengths and challenges. Protect my child from those that wish to hurt or take advantage of him/her. Protect me from envy and sadness when I see other people's "normal" children. Surround me with the people who will help me laugh when I need to; cry when it's healthy; pray every day; and remember that I'm not alone. Thank You, God, for the gift of this child. May I be worthy of raising him/her to his/her potential, to help him/her find love, life, joy, Judaism, happiness, success, friendship, and security, amen.

## On Day of Child's Bar/Bat Mitzvah

**We** thank You, our God, for the great joy that has come to us today, when we see our son/daughter take upon himself/herself the responsibility of Torah and Jewish life. May it serve him/her well, for lengthy days and health, blessing and success, life and peace. Today he/she merited receiving a holy spark from Heaven to lead him/her on the right path so he/she will grow steadily in good deeds and become inspired in a life of Torah.

*Please, God, help our son/daughter to always overcome his/her negative drives with all that is positive within him/her, and may he/she become an upright person, an honest person, a person of integrity and kindness and Torah values.*

*May he/she revere You and always find favor and good understanding in Your eyes and in the eyes of all people, and may we derive abundant nachas from him/her. May it be Your will that, just as You have been benevolent to us up until now, and have helped us raise our son/daughter until today, so may You show us compassion and not withhold Your kindness from us in the future. Thus we will be privileged to raise this son/daughter of ours, [as well as our other child(ren)], to Torah and good deeds in abundance and honor. Amen!*

## On Day of Child's Wedding

**God,** today is a day I've waited for and wondered about for many years — the day of marrying off a child, of walking that child down to the chuppah. I stand here before You with awe, gratitude, joy, love, and hope. You chose our child's soulmate, and now we will watch them join their lives together to create the next link in the chain of our family and faith. With tears we ask You to shower them with all Your blessings. May they be able to join together as one. Open the floodgates of grace and *kindness for them — that they may always delight in each other. May they create a happy and serene life together, free of argument or strife, of competition or envy. May this bond that they're creating under the chuppah be one that is everlasting and strong. Grant them livelihood, healthy children, and every blessing that we hope for them from the depths of our hearts. May this beautiful and auspicious moment be a symbol for the rest of their lives together, amen.*

*May this bond that they're creating under the chuppah be one that is everlasting and strong.*

# To Say at The Gravesite of a Loved One

Often we go to visit a gravesite, and are stumped as to what exactly to do or say there. Jewish customs at a gravesite include lighting a yahrtzeit candle and placing a stone on top of the headstone. The candle represents a soul, as the verse in Proverbs (20:27) states, "For the soul of a man is like the candle of God." A flame is like the spiritual part of the candle; it strives upward while everything else pulls downward. A stone at the site represents the eternity of our loved one. Stones are eternal — unlike flowers, they never wither or die. So too, Judaism teaches that our loved one's spirit, and the effect he or she has had on the world, is forever. In addition, it is not a Jewish practice to pray directly to our loved one. We only pray to God. It is, however, an accepted practice to talk to our loved one, and to beseech him or her to "intercede" with God in the heavens to plead for our requests. Many also recite Psalm 91, below, as an expression of God protecting us and being with us in our pain.

**יֹשֵׁב** בְּסֵתֶר עֶלְיוֹן, בְּצֵל שַׁדַּי יִתְלוֹנָן. אֹמַר לַיְיָ מַחְסִי וּמְצוּדָתִי, אֱלֹהַי אֶבְטַח בּוֹ. כִּי הוּא יַצִּילְךָ מִפַּח יָקוּשׁ, מִדֶּבֶר הַוּוֹת. בְּאֶבְרָתוֹ יָסֶךְ לָךְ, וְתַחַת כְּנָפָיו תֶּחְסֶה, צִנָּה וְסֹחֵרָה אֲמִתּוֹ. לֹא תִירָא מִפַּחַד לָיְלָה, מֵחֵץ יָעוּף יוֹמָם. מִדֶּבֶר בָּאֹפֶל יַהֲלֹךְ, מִקֶּטֶב יָשׁוּד צָהֳרָיִם. יִפֹּל מִצִּדְּךָ אֶלֶף וּרְבָבָה מִימִינֶךָ, אֵלֶיךָ לֹא יִגָּשׁ. רַק בְּעֵינֶיךָ תַבִּיט, וְשִׁלֻּמַת רְשָׁעִים תִּרְאֶה. כִּי אַתָּה יְיָ מַחְסִי, עֶלְיוֹן שַׂמְתָּ מְעוֹנֶךָ. לֹא תְאֻנֶּה אֵלֶיךָ רָעָה, וְנֶגַע לֹא יִקְרַב בְּאָהֳלֶךָ. כִּי מַלְאָכָיו יְצַוֶּה לָּךְ, לִשְׁמָרְךָ בְּכָל דְּרָכֶיךָ. עַל כַּפַּיִם יִשָּׂאוּנְךָ, פֶּן תִּגֹּף בָּאֶבֶן רַגְלֶךָ. עַל שַׁחַל וָפֶתֶן תִּדְרֹךְ, תִּרְמֹס כְּפִיר וְתַנִּין. כִּי בִי חָשַׁק וַאֲפַלְּטֵהוּ, אֲשַׂגְּבֵהוּ כִּי יָדַע שְׁמִי. יִקְרָאֵנִי וְאֶעֱנֵהוּ, עִמּוֹ אָנֹכִי בְצָרָה, אֲחַלְּצֵהוּ וַאֲכַבְּדֵהוּ. אֹרֶךְ יָמִים אַשְׂבִּיעֵהוּ, וְאַרְאֵהוּ בִּישׁוּעָתִי. אֹרֶךְ יָמִים אַשְׂבִּיעֵהוּ, וְאַרְאֵהוּ בִּישׁוּעָתִי.

**Yoshev** b'sayter elyon, b'tzel Shaddai yit-lonan. Omar la-Adonoi mach-si u-m'tzudati, Elohai ev-tach bo. Ki hu yatzil-cha mi-pach yakush mi-dever ha-vot. B'evrato yasech lach, v'tachat k'nafav techeseh, tzinah v'socherah amito. Lo tira mi-pachad laila, may-chaytz ya-uf yomam. Mi-dever ba-ofel ya-haloch, mi-ketev yashud tza-ha-rayim. Yipol mi-tzidcha elef u-revava mi-minecha, ay-lecha lo yi-gash. Rak b'aynecha tabit, v'shi-lumat resha-im tir-eh. Ki Ata Adonoi mach-si, elyon samta m'o-necha. Lo t'u-neh ay-lecha ra-ah, v'nega lo yikrav b'ahalecha. Ki malachav y'tzaveh lach li-shmarcha b'chol d'ra-checha. Al kapayim yi-sa-uncha pen tigof ba-even raglecha. Al shachal va-feten ti-droch tir-mos kfir v'tanin. Ki vi cha-shak va-a-fal-tayhu, asag-vayhu ki yada shmi. Yik-ra-ayni v'eh-eh-nayhu, imo

Various Prayers 173

*anochi b'tzara, achal-tzay-hu v'achab-day-hu. Orech yamim as-bi-ayhu v'ar-ay-hu bi-shu-ah-ti.*

**He** *Who resides in the shadow of the Exalted One, he'll dwell in the shadow of God. I will say to God: "You are my safe place and my fortress, my God, and I will trust in Him." For He will save you from a dangerous trap, from a debilitating plague. With His wings He will cover you, and you will be covered beneath His wings. Shield and armor are His truth. Don't fear the fright of night, or the arrow that flies by day; from the plague that walks in darkness, from the destructive force that destroys in the afternoon. A thousand could camp at your side, and a myriad at your right — but they won't come near to you. You will glance with your eyes and see the comeuppance of the wicked. Because "You, my God, are my safe place," and you have made the Exalted One your home. No evil will come to you, and plagues will not get near your tent. He will command His angels to [assist] you, to guard over you in all your ways. They will carry you on their palms, that your foot not hit a stone. You'll step over lion and venomous snake, you'll trample the lion cub and snake. He has desired Me, and I'll deliver him — I will elevate him for he has known My name. He will call Me and I will answer him, I am with him in his sorrow; I will release him and honor him. I'll satisfy him with long life and show him My salvation.*

Dear God, here I am at the gravesite of my beloved friend/relative. I stand here in a state of reverence and with a mixture of sadness, peace, grief, and respect. I have strong feelings of closeness and at the same time, the gulf of distance is incredibly vast. I put my trust in You, God, as the protective shade for my loved one. I feel better as I envision Your protective force shielding his/her soul, as he/she is at peace — unaffected by the difficulties and vicissitudes of this world down here. I imagine my loved one praying for me and interceding on my behalf, and in response, You, God, commanding angels to watch over me wherever I go. In the merit of my loved one, protect me and those I care for from harm. I know You are with me when I miss him/her, and when bad things happen to me in my life. With You at my side, God, I don't need to fear pain, loss, or difficulty.

---

I HAVE THE STRONG FEELINGS OF CLOSENESS AND AT THE SAME TIME, THE GULF OF DISTANCE IS INCREDIBLY VAST.

---

# ISRAEL AND SPIRITUALITY

## Welcoming Holidays

**Dear** God, as we welcome the holiday of _____, I turn to You for inspiration and personal request. Help our family celebrate this holiday with pride and joy. Help us to prepare for it happily. [May our children connect to the meaning and may they form happy memories that will stay with them forever.] Help us to observe this holiday correctly and meaningfully.

**Rosh Hashanah**: Help us to remember that You are our King and judge, and gift us with a sweet new year.

**Yom Kippur**: Help us to regret and fix our misdeeds, and to live out the upcoming year in a better and more mature way.

**Sukkot**: Help us to take great joy in the fact that You protected us in the desert in the past, and will always continue to shield and protect us as a people.

**Chanukah**: Help us to always be proud of our Judaism, and to live that pride daily, and to remember that miracles do happen and that there's always a light in the darkest of times.

**Tu B'shvat**: Help us to remember that You renew the agriculture every year, and to be grateful for our bounty.

**Purim**: Help us to remember the miracle of Jewish survival, and to renew our commitment to celebrate our identity as Jews daily.

**Passover**: Help us to thank You joyfully for taking us out of Egypt and creating our nation, and to pass along that joy and gratitude to the next generation.

**Shavuot**: Help us to remember how blessed we are to be the Chosen People, to be a light unto the nations, and to be grateful every day for the gift of Torah.

## Safety for Israel and The Israeli Soldiers

### Dear God,

Protect the residents of the Land of Israel from terror, fear, and danger. Foil the attempts of evil people to *destroy and harm us. Gift the army with wisdom and courage to defend our people and our Land. Protect the soldiers of the IDF that they may return home quickly to their families safe and sound. Allow our fellow brothers and sisters in the Land of Israel to work, pray, study Torah, celebrate and observe Judaism with pride, and live their lives without anxiety and worry. Bring peace to Your holy land quickly, amen.*

## Rosh Chodesh — a New Jewish Month

Rosh Chodesh is the day or days which herald a new Jewish month. It is uniquely associated with women, who share their monthly renewal with the moon. When the Jewish people sinned at the Golden Calf, the women refused to participate, and were gifted with the semi-holiday in return. It is the perfect opportunity to pause, reflect, thank God for the blessings of the previous month, and ask Him for new opportunities in the upcoming month.

### Dear God,

*May You bring this new month upon us for goodness and for blessing. May You give us long life — a life of peace, a life of goodness, a life of blessing, a life of livelihood, a life of physical strength, a life in which we revere Heaven and fear sin, a life free of shame and embarrassment, a life of wealth and honor, a life in which we have a love for Torah and reverence of heaven, a life in which God fulfills* all the wishes of our heart for the good, amen! May God renew this month for us and for all of Israel in life, peace, joy, happiness, and consolation, amen!

## For Help on One's Spiritual Journey

**Dear God,**

I'm on a path — a journey — toward You. My spiritual journey takes twists and turns. Sometimes it's two steps forward and one step back. Sometimes it's one step forward and three steps back. Sometimes I feel Your presence so strongly, I could cry; but other times, I wonder where You've gone. It can be so hard to perceive Your hand in my life. Help me to see Your presence wherever I go. Help me to pray and talk to You in my successes and failures. Help me to study and fulfill Torah to my best ability. Send me teachers and mentors who will inspire me and trust me on my path. Send me peers and friends who understand and support me in my journey. Protect my heart from hurtful and disparaging comments and attitudes from those who do not understand. Help me to ignore and even forgive those comments. Inspire me in my path to keep trying a bit more than yesterday and to continually climb my ladder of growth at the right pace. Don't let me become arrogant, discouraged, or complacent on the journey. Help me to remember that You are not comparing me to anyone else; only to my own potential. Help me to love myself while always trying harder. Help me not to judge others who are not on a similar journey of growth. Help me to portray my Judaism beautifully and sensitively to people in my life who may not understand. Allow me to grow each day and not be static in my relationships, and thus, may I be a source of inspiration for others and have no cause for regrets. Allow me to be proud of my successes and grateful to all those who helped me reach them. "Show me, God, Your way, and guide me on a straight path…" Amen.

# At the Western Wall and Other Holy Sites

**Dear God,**

I stand before You at this holy site — a place that has deep meaning for Jews the world over. Here, Your presence is felt more strongly than in other places and the concentration of Your presence is more intense. As I stand at the holy place, God, I invoke the merit of our ancestors who stood here before me, and of all the Jewish people, my fellow brothers and sisters, who traveled to this place to pray and connect to You. Please, God, in this moment, have compassion on me and inspire me to become a better person. Grant me the privilege of making amends for my mistakes. Let me attain love, kindness, and compassion in Your eyes and the eyes of all people. Let them forgive me for anything I've done. Instill in my heart the will to serve You. Help me to pray with devotion and intent. Gift me with strength to live properly and provide us with a generous livelihood. May the Torah always be a part of my family's life, and may all my children and descendants be proud and devoted Jews. Specifically, have compassion on [Hebrew name ben/bat Hebrew name] for _____. May the words of my mouth and the thoughts of my heart be favorable before You, God, our rock and redeemer.

## OTHER VARIOUS PRAYERS

### When Hearing of a Tragedy

**Dear God,**

I've been struggling since hearing of the news about _____. It's so hard for me to understand how these things happen. But God, I recognize, in my mind if not emotionally, that You have Your ways and Your plans that are unfathomable to me.

I can't control evil, but I can fight it by bringing a little more goodness into the world. And so God, I would like to use these moments to show faith and compassion by praying.

*Please, God, bring comfort to the innocent families of the victims. Please bring healing to the injured. Help all of them to heal in their bodies and minds, and to heal in their faith in the essential goodness of this world. Help them and us heal in understanding that while there is evil in this world, it is mostly a good place with mostly good people. Restore their faith in humanity. Help them to rebuild normal lives.*

*And please God, assist the law enforcement professionals in ending evil. Bring justice, that we may live in peace and joy, and may we remember You in those moments as well.*

## Prayer for Peace

**God,** *please help our world to be more peaceful. I pray not just for peace, but for lots of other things that go along with it: goodness, blessing, life, mutual respect, kindness, compassion. Bless us with Your special, peaceful light — with Your holiness. It hurts me so much that people misunderstand each other so badly in families and communities, and that there is so much gossip, envy, and pride. I imagine it must pain You too, God. Let us be able to get along with friends and family, to put aside our petty disagreements, to swallow our arrogance, to control our emotions, to display integrity, class, and dignity in our relationships. Let us remember that difficult people are* there to teach us these things and to cultivate our patience, compassion, and forgiveness. Allow us to understand one another and share our values in making this world a better place — to remember that loving our neighbors will build bridges, connections, and mutual respect.

Let us remember that difficult people are there to teach us these things and to cultivate our patience, compassion, and forgiveness.

## Aging with Grace

*composed by Sarah Moses Spero*

**Help** *me to remember*

that we were once young — and thought we knew better, too

that aging does not guarantee the insight of our words nor the wisdom of our actions

that we must be patient so that we can appreciate the naivete and youth of those who are not

**Help** *me to remember*

that though children are the center of our lives, we are not the center of theirs

that we made our own mistakes and must allow our children to make theirs that others may have valid and worthy opinions though we do not necessarily agree

**Help** *me to remember*

that wisdom and patience are ongoing and must be nurtured at every age

that forgiveness, though often Divine, can be given and shared

that we must find ways to be grateful and express gratitude to those around us because we owe it to You

**Help** *me to remember*

that we must find ways to fill our lives with meaning, for no one else will

that we must find ways to create our own happiness, for no one else will

that we must find ways to fill our hearts with blessing, for no one else will

**Help** *me to remember*

that we not become selfish or self-centered as our dependence on others grows

that sometimes we may have to lend an ear and hold a tongue

that we not become so set in our ways that we are not open to new and fresh ideas

**Help** *me to remember*

that when it is time to step aside we will do so with kindness, humility, and grace that "young" is neither a title nor an entitlement — and neither is "old"

that memories are personal and should be enjoyed and remembered privately — again and again

**Help** me to remember

that we must be ever-mindful of our surroundings and not test the patience of others

that we find the courage to reject bitterness and regret that may want to become our friends

that the weakness of our bodies does not define the strength of our character

**Help** me to remember

that dignity is a gift we must cherish, for the time may come when other hands will aid

that compassion, modesty, and understanding will take on new meaning

that loss, pain, and loneliness must be respected for they will be our constant companion

**Help** me to remember

that sometimes others may make decisions for us that we do not like

that both love and pain may have been part of that process

that though the action may not have been our choice, our reaction is

**Help** *me to remember*

*that tomorrow will be a new day, a better day, a day filled with promise and future and that the decision is mine*

*Amen.*

# Forgiveness

רִ**בּוֹנוֹ** שֶׁל עוֹלָם, הֲרֵינִי מוֹחֵל לְכָל מִי שֶׁהִכְעִיס וְהִקְנִיט אוֹתִי, אוֹ שֶׁחָטָא כְּנֶגְדִּי, בֵּין בְּגוּפִי בֵּין בְּמָמוֹנִי, בֵּין בִּכְבוֹדִי בֵּין בְּכָל אֲשֶׁר לִי, בֵּין בְּאֹנֶס בֵּין בְּרָצוֹן, בֵּין בְּשׁוֹגֵג בֵּין בְּמֵזִיד, בֵּין בְּדִבּוּר בֵּין בְּמַעֲשֶׂה, בֵּין בְּמַחֲשָׁבָה בֵּין בְּהִרְהוּר, בֵּין בְּגִלְגּוּל זֶה בֵּין בְּגִלְגּוּל אַחֵר, לְכָל בַּר יִשְׂרָאֵל, וְלֹא יֵעָנֵשׁ שׁוּם אָדָם בְּסִבָּתִי. יְהִי רָצוֹן מִלְּפָנֶיךָ, יְיָ אֱלֹהַי וֵאלֹהֵי אֲבוֹתַי, שֶׁלֹּא אֶחֱטָא עוֹד, וּמַה שֶּׁחָטָאתִי לְפָנֶיךָ מְחוֹק בְּרַחֲמֶיךָ הָרַבִּים, אֲבָל לֹא עַל יְדֵי יִסּוּרִים וָחֳלָיִים רָעִים. יִהְיוּ לְרָצוֹן אִמְרֵי פִי וְהֶגְיוֹן לִבִּי לְפָנֶיךָ, יְיָ צוּרִי וְגֹאֲלִי.

**Ribono** shel olam, harayni mochel l'chol mi she-hich-is v'hik-nit oti, o she-chata k'negdi, bayn b'gufi, bayn b'mamoni, bayn bi-chvodi, bayn b'chol asher li, bayn b'ones, bayn b'ratzon, bayn b'shogeg, bayn b'may-zid, bayn b'dibur, bayn b'ma-aseh, bayn b'machshavah, bayn b'hirhur, bayn b'gilgul zeh, bayn b'gilgul acher, l'chol bar Yisrael, v'lo yay-anesh shum adam b'sibati. Y'hi ratzon mil-fanecha, Adonoi Elohai vay-lohay

Various Prayers

avotai, she-lo echeta od, u-ma she-chatati l'fanecha m'chok b'rachamecha ha-rabim, aval lo al y'day yisurim v'chalayim ra-im. Yi-hi-yu l'ratzon imray fi v'hegyon libi l'fanecha, Adonoi tzuri v'goali.

**God,** I hereby forgive all those that have angered and hurt me, whether it affected my body, my money, my honor, or anything of mine; whether by accident, on purpose, or against their will; whether with speech, deed, or thought; whether in this life or a previous life; I forgive all, and hope that no person be punished because of me. [And I specifically forgive _____ for_____.] God, I truly hope that I do not repeat the mistakes of my past. Whatever mistakes I have made, please erase from my record in Your great mercy and don't punish me because of them. I sincerely hope that You hear and listen to this prayer. Amen.

## For Self To Remain Healthy:

**God,** in Your great compassion please give me strength, health, and ability; energy and vigor of every part of my body. Please don't let any weakness or aches and pains come over me. May we be happy and healthy in order to be good Jews. Save us from any mishap or difficulty. Give us long, happy, and healthy lives. Fill our days and years with goodness and joy. Save me and all my family members from any pain or difficulty, and may we have contentment and serenity all the days of our lives, and be able to live them out with vigor and energy in order to serve You well, amen.

## For Others Who Are Ill:

**God,** please heal and bring recovery, quickly and easily, to [insert name of ill person with the formula (Hebrew name) ben/bat (mother's Hebrew name)]. Help him/her to regain all his/her capacities, whether physical, mental, or emotional. Allow him/her to grow old in joy and health, and be able to enjoy all that life has to offer, and to reach his/her potential, together with all of the rest of our nation.

## To Speak Positively of Others

**רבונו** שֶׁל עוֹלָם, יְהִי רָצוֹן מִלְּפָנֶיךָ, אֵל רַחוּם וְחַנּוּן, שֶׁתְּזַכֵּנִי הַיּוֹם וּבְכָל יוֹם לִשְׁמוֹר פִּי וּלְשׁוֹנִי מִלָּשׁוֹן-הָרַע וּרְכִילוּת וּמְקַבְּלָתָם. וְאֶזָּהֵר מִלְּדַבֵּר אֲפִלּוּ עַל אִישׁ יְחִידִי, וְכָל שֶׁכֵּן מִלְּדַבֵּר עַל כְּלַל יִשְׂרָאֵל אוֹ עַל חֵלֶק מֵהֶם. וְכָל שֶׁכֵּן מִלְהִתְרַעֵם

**Various Prayers** 187

עַל מִדּוֹתָיו שֶׁל הַקָּדוֹשׁ־בָּרוּךְ־הוּא. וְאֶזָּהֵר מִלְּדַבֵּר דִּבְרֵי שֶׁקֶר, חֲנֻפָּה, לֵצָנוּת, מַחֲלֹקֶת, כַּעַס, גַּאֲוָה, אוֹנָאַת־דְּבָרִים, הַלְבָּנַת־פָּנִים, וְכָל דְּבָרִים אֲסוּרִים. וְזַכֵּנִי שֶׁלֹּא לְדַבֵּר כִּי אִם דָּבָר הַצָּרִיךְ לְעִנְיָנֵי גוּפִי אוֹ נַפְשִׁי. וְשֶׁיִּהְיוּ כָּל מַעֲשַׂי לְשֵׁם שָׁמַיִם.

**Ribono** shel olam, y'hi ratzon mil-fanecha, El rachum v'chanun, she-t'zakayni ha-yom u-v'chol yom li-shmor pi u-leshoni mi-lashon hara u-rechi-lut u-mi-kabalatam. V'ezaher mi-ledaber afilu al ish ye-chidi v'chol she-ken mi-ledaber al klal Yisrael oh al chelek may-hem. V'chol she-ken mi-le-hit-ra-em al midotav shel ha-Kadosh Baruch Hu. V'ezaher mi-ledaber divray sheker, chanufah, lay-tza-nut, mach-loket, ka-as, ga-ava, ona-at devarim, hal-banat panim, v'chol devarim asurim. V'zakayni she-lo l'daber ki im davar ha-tzarich l'inyanay gufi oh nafshi. V'she-yi-hi-yu kol ma-asai l'shem shamayim.

**Master** of the universe, may it be Your will, compassionate God, that You give me the privilege, today and every day, to hold my tongue from speaking gossip and slander — and to not believe those words when they are spoken to me. May I succeed in being careful even when speaking about one individual, and of course when speaking of the entire Jewish people or a segment of them. Even more so, help me refrain from complaining about Your ways, God. May I succeed in being careful to stay away from lies, false flattery, stupidities, fighting, anger, arrogance, verbal abuse, embarrassing others, and all other forms of speech that You don't allow. Give me the privilege to use my power of speech for positivity — to build people and create positive change whether for body or soul. May all my deeds be for a positive purpose.

*Give me the privilege to use my power of speech for positivity — to build people and create positive change whether for body or soul.*

# For Safe Travels

יְהִי רָצוֹן מִלְפָנֶיךָ יְיָ אֱלֹהֵינוּ וֵאלֹהֵי אֲבוֹתֵינוּ, שֶׁתּוֹלִיכֵנוּ לְשָׁלוֹם וְתַצְעִידֵנוּ לְשָׁלוֹם וְתַדְרִיכֵנוּ לְשָׁלוֹם, וְתַגִּיעֵנוּ לִמְחוֹז חֶפְצֵנוּ לְחַיִּים וּלְשִׂמְחָה וּלְשָׁלוֹם, וְתַצִּילֵנוּ מִכַּף כָּל אוֹיֵב וְאוֹרֵב, וּמִכָּל מִינֵי פֻּרְעָנִיּוֹת הַמִּתְרַגְּשׁוֹת לָבוֹא לָעוֹלָם וְתִשְׁלַח בְּרָכָה בְּמַעֲשֵׂה יָדֵינוּ וְתִתְּנֵנוּ לְחֵן וּלְחֶסֶד וּלְרַחֲמִים בְּעֵינֶיךָ וּבְעֵינֵי כָל רֹאֵינוּ, וְתִשְׁמַע קוֹל תַּחֲנוּנֵינוּ, כִּי אֵל שׁוֹמֵעַ תְּפִלָּה וְתַחֲנוּן אָתָּה: בָּרוּךְ אַתָּה יְיָ, שׁוֹמֵעַ תְּפִלָּה.

**Y'hi** ratzon mil-fanecha, Adonoi Elohaynu vay-lohay avo-taynu, she-tolichaynu l'shalom, v'ta-tzidaynu l'shalom, v'tadri-chaynu l'shalom, v'tagi-aynu li-m'choz chef-tzaynu l'chaim u-l'simcha u-l'shalom. V'ta-tzilaynu mi-kaf kol oyev v'orayv, u-mi-kol minay pur-aniyot ha-mit-ragshot lavo l'olam. V'tishlach bracha b'chol ma-asay ya-daynu, v'tit-naynu l'chayn u-l'chesed u-l'rachamim, b'aynaynu u-v'aynay kol ro-ay-nu, v'tish-ma kol ta-cha-nu-naynu, ki El shomaya tefila v'tachanun Ata. Baruch Ata Adonoi, shomaya tefila.

**May** it be Your will, God, our God and the God of our ancestors, that You lead us in peace, and guide our footsteps in peace, and show the way in peace, and may we reach our destination in life, joy, and peace. Save us from enemies, dangers, thieves, and wild animals along the way, and from any kind of mishap that befall people and come to the world. Send blessing to all our endeavors, and allow us to experience favor, kindness, and compassion in the eyes of all who encounter us, and hear our prayers, for You are the God Who hears prayers and requests. Blessed are You, God, Who hears prayer.

## After Having a Bad Dream

**God,** I had a dream last night and I don't know what it means. I am feeling unnerved and scared by this dream. I know that dreams are Yours, and I therefore turn to You with these feelings. Please, may all my dreams, whether about myself or others, be good ones. If they are good, strengthen them, make them come true, and let them endure. But if they need healing, please heal them just as You've healed others throughout our history. You have the ability to transform curse into blessing, and thus may You transform all my dreams for goodness. Protect me, be kind to me, and accept my words, amen.

# To Find Lost Objects

אֱלָהָא דְמֵאִיר עֲנֵנִי, אֱלָהָא דְמֵאִיר עֲנֵנִי, אֱלָהָא דְמֵאִיר עֲנֵנִי. בִּזְכוּת הַצְּדָקָה שֶׁאֲנִי נוֹדֵב לְעִילוּי נִשְׁמַת רַבִּי מֵאִיר בַּעַל הַנֵּס, זְכוּתוֹ יָגֵן עָלֵינוּ, לִמְצוֹא אֶת הָאֲבֵדָה שֶׁאָבַדְתִּי.

**Elaka** d'Meir anayni, Elaka d'Meir anayni, Elaka d'Meir anayni. Bi-z'chut ha-tzedakah she-ani nodev l'iluy nishmat Rabi Meir Ba-al Ha-nes, z'chuto yagen alaynu, lim-tzo et ha-avayda she-avad'ti.

**God** of Meir, answer me, God of Meir, answer me, God of Meir, answer me. In the merit of the charity I am donating for the elevation of the soul of Rabbi Meir Ba-al Ha-nes, may his merits protect us, may I find what I have lost.

אָמַר רַבִּי בִּנְיָמִין, הַכֹּל בְּחֶזְקַת סוּמִין, עַד שֶׁהַקָּדוֹשׁ בָּרוּךְ הוּא מֵאִיר אֶת עֵינֵיהֶם.

**Amar** Rabbi Binyamin, ha-kol b'chez-kat sumin, ad she-ha-Kadosh Baruch Hu may-ir et aynayhem.

**Rabbi** Binyanim said, "Everyone is like a blind person — until the holy One, blessed is He, enlightens their eyes."

*[At this point one should donate some money to charity — it can be any amount.]*

## Dealing with Suffering

**God,** as I go through life, I find myself in a very difficult challenge right now. It is hard for me to understand why I am experiencing this suffering. Am I such a bad person, God, that I don't deserve the peace and serenity others seem to have? Sometimes, God, I don't feel strong enough to prevail in this dark time. But maybe God, You are testing me — to see how I will react. Maybe this experience has the potential to bring out in me new strengths and a deeper sense of self that I never knew possible. Maybe this challenge is there to help me develop compassion and sensitivity toward others who are suffering. Please God, don't make my challenge so difficult. Help me to feel Your loving presence in these dark times. Help me to remember that prayer centers and comforts me. Surround me with people to love and support me. Save me from fear and worry about the future and just focus on today. Let me remember to laugh and to love. Let me see the silver lining. Let me give myself permission to grieve and to cry — and then to move on. Help me to accept my suffering with serenity and peace. Help me to stop railing against that which I cannot change. Gift me with the strength I never knew I had to pull through, to live life, to continue, and even to grow from my suffering.

# Psalms

*Psalms are the go-to prayer for every occasion of the human experience. Most of the one hundred and fifty psalms in the Book of Psalms, which is part of the Tanach, are songs and prayers written by King David. King David experienced the highest of highs and the lowest of lows. He was persecuted, pursued, and hated by beloved family members. He was misunderstood and shunned by his own family. He was the king of the Jewish people and one of its humblest, most noble leaders. And throughout every triumph and travail, King David turned to God in song. The Book of Psalms is that legacy. It is said that if one recites these psalms, even if she does not understand them, she is linking herself to the spirit of King David. Below are five of the most commonly recited psalms for various occasions.*

---

AND THROUGHOUT EVERY TRIUMPH AND TRAVAIL, KING DAVID TURNED TO GOD IN SONG. THE BOOK OF PSALMS IS THAT LEGACY.

---

# Psalm 23

*King David composed this prayer when he was a lone fugitive in a forest, starved to the point of death, and God prepared delicious sweet grass to sustain him. It is the universal prayer of faith in dark times.*

מִזְמוֹר לְדָוִד יְיָ רֹעִי לֹא אֶחְסָר: בִּנְאוֹת דֶּשֶׁא יַרְבִּיצֵנִי עַל־מֵי מְנֻחוֹת יְנַהֲלֵנִי: נַפְשִׁי יְשׁוֹבֵב יַנְחֵנִי בְמַעְגְּלֵי־צֶדֶק לְמַעַן שְׁמוֹ: גַּם כִּי־אֵלֵךְ בְּגֵיא צַלְמָוֶת לֹא־אִירָא רָע כִּי־אַתָּה עִמָּדִי שִׁבְטְךָ וּמִשְׁעַנְתֶּךָ הֵמָּה יְנַחֲמֻנִי: תַּעֲרֹךְ לְפָנַי שֻׁלְחָן נֶגֶד צֹרְרָי דִּשַּׁנְתָּ בַשֶּׁמֶן רֹאשִׁי כּוֹסִי רְוָיָה: אַךְ טוֹב וָחֶסֶד יִרְדְּפוּנִי כָּל־יְמֵי חַיָּי וְשַׁבְתִּי בְּבֵית־יְיָ לְאֹרֶךְ יָמִים:

**Mizmor** l'David. Adonoi ro-i lo echsar. Bin-ot desheh yar-bi-tzayni, al may minuchot y'na-ha-layni.

*Nafshi y'shovev, yan-chayni b'maglay tzedek l'ma-an sh'mo. Gam ki ay-lech b'gay tzal-mavet, lo ira ra ki Ata imadi. Shiv-t'cha u-mishantecha hayma y'nachamuni. Ta-aroch l'fanai shulchan neged tzo-r'rai, dishanta ba-shemen roshi kosi revaya. Ach tov vachesed yir-d'funi kol y'may chai-yai, v'shavti b'vet Adonoi l'orech yamim.*

**A** *song of David. God is my shepherd, I won't lack. He will bring me to lush fields, He will lead me to calm waters. My soul will calm; He will guide me through righteous paths for His name's sake. Although I may walk in the valley of the shadow of death, I will not be afraid, because You are with me. Your rod and Your staff — they comfort me. You will set a table for me before my enemies; You have anointed my head with oil; my cup overflows. Only goodness and kindness will pursue me all the days of my life, and I will dwell in the house of God for many long days.*

God, there are times in life when things seem really bleak. But the thought of Your presence is a comfort to me. No matter what is going on — You can turn it around. You always have a better tomorrow awaiting us. Even though I can't see You, You are there helping me succeed. You can turn any situation around in an instant. You will help me survive and emerge victorious. I am optimistic and full of faith that I will live a long and happy life, full of goodness, with You, God, at my side.

# Psalm 30

This is a prayer of thanksgiving and faith composed by David at the pinnacle of our national pride: the inauguration of our Holy Temple in Jerusalem. In it, King David expresses both gratitude to God for His blessings and a prayerful hope that His kindnesses always continue. This is a psalm that is often chosen when begging God for relief or healing.

מִזְמוֹר שִׁיר חֲנֻכַּת הַבַּיִת לְדָוִד: אֲרוֹמִמְךָ יְיָ כִּי דִלִּיתָנִי וְלֹא־שִׂמַּחְתָּ אֹיְבַי לִי: יְיָ אֱלֹהָי שִׁוַּעְתִּי אֵלֶיךָ וַתִּרְפָּאֵנִי: יְיָ הֶעֱלִיתָ מִן־שְׁאוֹל נַפְשִׁי חִיִּיתַנִי מִיָּרְדִי בוֹר: זַמְּרוּ לַיהוָה חֲסִידָיו וְהוֹדוּ לְזֵכֶר קָדְשׁוֹ: כִּי רֶגַע בְּאַפּוֹ חַיִּים בִּרְצוֹנוֹ בָּעֶרֶב יָלִין בֶּכִי וְלַבֹּקֶר רִנָּה: וַאֲנִי אָמַרְתִּי בְשַׁלְוִי בַּל־אֶמּוֹט לְעוֹלָם: יְיָ בִּרְצוֹנְךָ הֶעֱמַדְתָּה לְהַרְרִי עֹז הִסְתַּרְתָּ פָנֶיךָ הָיִיתִי נִבְהָל: אֵלֶיךָ יְיָ אֶקְרָא וְאֶל־אֲדֹנָי אֶתְחַנָּן: מַה־בֶּצַע בְּדָמִי בְּרִדְתִּי אֶל־שָׁחַת הֲיוֹדְךָ עָפָר הֲיַגִּיד אֲמִתֶּךָ: שְׁמַע־יְיָ וְחָנֵּנִי יְיָ הֱיֵה עֹזֵר לִי: הָפַכְתָּ מִסְפְּדִי לְמָחוֹל לִי פִּתַּחְתָּ שַׂקִּי וַתְּאַזְּרֵנִי שִׂמְחָה: לְמַעַן יְזַמֶּרְךָ כָבוֹד וְלֹא יִדֹּם יְיָ אֱלֹהַי לְעוֹלָם אוֹדֶךָּ:

**Mizmor** shir chanukat ha-bayit l'David. Aro-mim-cha Adonoi ki di-li-tani v'lo simachta oy-vai li. Adonoi Elohai shi-vati ay-lecha va-tir-pa-ayni. Adonoi he-elita min sh'ol nafshi chi-yi-tani mi-yordi bor. Zamru la-Adonoi chasidav v'hodu l'zecher kad-sho. Ki rega b'apo, chaim bir-tzono, ba-erev yalin bechi v'la-boker rina. Va-ani amarti b'shalvi, bal emot l'olam. Adonoi bir-tzoncha he-e-mad'ta l'ha-reri oz, his-tarta panecha hayiti niv-hal. Ay-lecha Adonoi ekra v'el Adonoi et-chanan. Mah betza b'dami b'rid'ti el shachat, ha-yod-cha afar, ha-yagid ami-techa. Shema Adonoi v'cha-nayni, Adonoi he-yay ozer li. Hafach-ta mis-p'di l'machol li, pi-tach-ta saki va-t'az-rayni simcha. L'ma-an y'za-mercha kavod v'lo yidom, Adonoi Elohai l'olam odeka.

**A *hymn***, *song of the inauguration of the Temple by David. I will raise You up, God, for You have saved me, and You have not allowed my enemies to gloat over me. God, my God, I hoped to You and You healed me! God has lifted me from the lowest depths of my soul, and has revived me from my descent to the deepest pit. God's pious ones will sing to Him; and will give praise at the mention of His holiness. For his anger is but a moment; He desires life; in the evening one lies down crying, but in the morning — a song of joy! I have said in my serene complacency, "I will never falter!" God, only through Your favor have You supported my greatness with strength — if You'd hide Your face, I'd be panic-stricken! To You, God, I will call, and to God I will plead. What good is my blood if I descend to the netherworld? Will the dust thank You? Will it tell of Your truth? Hear, God, and favor me; God, be a help for me. You have turned my mourning into dancing for me; You have undone my mourning clothes and dressed me in happiness! So that others may serenade You with glory and never be silent, I, my God, will forever thank You.*

God, when the Jews inaugurated the Temple, it was an amazing example of a beautiful and unexpected turnabout. Who would've believed that tiny, persecuted Israel could survive and thrive? God, help us, as well, to beat the odds. To survive against the statistics. Help us rise from the lowest depths of despair to the highest, most victorious heights! How will it help You, God, if we fail? If we succeed, we can sing Your praises and be so grateful for Your miracles. I need You, God! In my silliness I used to believe I could manage without Your help. But I can't! I depend on You for everything! Please, God, answer my prayers, and I will forever be grateful.

## Psalm 100

*This is a classic song of thanksgiving to God for the good things He bestows on us. May we never take them for granted. It also reminds us that Judaism, and our relationship with God, is supposed to be about joy — the underlying emotion that makes every relationship meaningful.*

---

IT ALSO REMINDS US THAT JUDAISM, AND OUR RELATIONSHIP WITH GOD, IS SUPPOSED TO BE ABOUT JOY — THE UNDERLYING EMOTION THAT MAKES EVERY RELATIONSHIP MEANINGFUL.

---

**מִזְמוֹר** לְתוֹדָה הָרִיעוּ לַיהוָה כָּל־הָאָרֶץ׃ עִבְדוּ אֶת־יְיָ בְּשִׂמְחָה בֹּאוּ לְפָנָיו בִּרְנָנָה׃ דְּעוּ כִּי יְיָ הוּא אֱלֹהִים הוּא עָשָׂנוּ וְלוֹ אֲנַחְנוּ עַמּוֹ וְצֹאן מַרְעִיתוֹ׃ בֹּאוּ שְׁעָרָיו בְּתוֹדָה חֲצֵרֹתָיו בִּתְהִלָּה הוֹדוּ לוֹ בָּרְכוּ שְׁמוֹ׃ כִּי־טוֹב יְיָ לְעוֹלָם חַסְדּוֹ וְעַד דֹּר וָדֹר אֱמוּנָתוֹ׃

**Mizmor** l'todah, ha-ri-u la-Adonoi kol ha-aretz. Ivdu et Adonoi b'simcha, bo-u l'fanav bir-nana. D'u ki Adonoi hu Elohim, hu asanu v'lo anachnu, amo v'tzon mar-i-to. Bo-u sh'arav b'todah, chatzay-rotav

*Psalms* 199

bi-tehilah, hodu lo barchu sh'mo. Ki tov Adonoi l'olam chas-do v'ad dor va-dor emunato.

**A** song of thanks, may the whole world call out to God. Serve God with joy; come before Him with happy song. Know that God is our God: He made us, and we are His; His nation, and the sheep of His flock. Come to His gates with gratitude; to His courtyard with praise. Praise Him and bless His name. For God is good; His kindnesses are forever; and His faithfulness is eternal.

God, I often turn to You when I need things, but I turn to You now in simple and honest gratitude. I am so grateful for all the good things You've done for me; for all the gifts You've bestowed upon me; for all the small miracles that happen in my life. I am so happy to be Yours! I'm so happy to be Jewish! Thank You, God, forever and ever.

## Psalm 121

*In this psalm we are reassured that God is always watching over us, when it's obvious and even when it's hard to tell. This psalm is appropriate to recite whenever we need God's help. It is my personal favorite whenever I turn to God.*

שִׁיר לַמַּעֲלוֹת אֶשָּׂא עֵינַי אֶל הֶהָרִים מֵאַיִן יָבֹא עֶזְרִי: עֶזְרִי מֵעִם יְיָ עֹשֵׂה שָׁמַיִם וָאָרֶץ: אַל יִתֵּן לַמּוֹט רַגְלֶךָ אַל יָנוּם שֹׁמְרֶךָ: הִנֵּה לֹא יָנוּם וְלֹא יִישָׁן שׁוֹמֵר יִשְׂרָאֵל: יְיָ שֹׁמְרֶךָ יְיָ צִלְּךָ עַל יַד יְמִינֶךָ: יוֹמָם הַשֶּׁמֶשׁ לֹא יַכֶּכָּה וְיָרֵחַ בַּלָּיְלָה: יְיָ

יִשְׁמָרְךָ מִכָּל רָע יִשְׁמֹר אֶת נַפְשֶׁךָ: יְיָ יִשְׁמָר צֵאתְךָ וּבוֹאֶךָ מֵעַתָּה וְעַד עוֹלָם:

**Shir** la-ma-alot. Esa ay-nai el he-harim may-ayin yavo ezri. Ezri may-im Adonoi, osay shamayim va-aretz. Al yitayn lamot rag-lecha, al yanum shomrecha. Hinay lo yanum v'lo yishan, shomer Yisrael. Adonoi shom-recha, Adonoi tzil-cha al yad y'minecha. Yomam ha-shemesh lo ya-keka v'yaray-ach ba-layla. Adonoi yish-marcha mi-kol ra, yishmor et nafshecha. Adonoi yishmor tzayt-cha u-vo-echa may-ata v'ad olam.

**A** song of ascents. I lift my eyes to the mountains — from where will my help come? My help is from God, Who makes heaven and earth. He will not allow your foot to stumble; your Guardian does not sleep. Behold, the Guardian of Israel neither slumbers nor sleeps. God is your guardian, and God is your protective shade at your right hand. The sun will not harm you by day, nor the moon by night. God will protect you from all evil; He will guard your soul. God will guard your goings and comings from now until forever.

God, in this confusing, turbulent world, it is so reassuring to know that You are a constant. You don't ever take a break and You don't ever get tired of helping us. We hire human watchmen and protectors, but You are our ultimate help. If I ever wonder who can help me in my difficulties, I will remember that You are always there, waiting for us to turn to You, watching over Your precious nation, and making sure we are okay. And with Your help, God, I know, with faith and serenity, that it will be okay. That is our assurance, and it will be ours for always.

*Psalms*

# Psalm 130

*This psalm is a short but heartfelt reminder that God is on our side and we can always turn to Him. No matter what mistakes we may have made in our lives, He will always forgive us when we are ready to repent.*

שִׁיר הַמַּעֲלוֹת מִמַּעֲמַקִּים קְרָאתִיךָ יְיָ: אֲדֹנָי שִׁמְעָה בְקוֹלִי תִּהְיֶינָה אָזְנֶיךָ קַשֻּׁבוֹת לְקוֹל תַּחֲנוּנָי: אִם עֲוֹנוֹת תִּשְׁמָר יָהּ אֲדֹנָי מִי יַעֲמֹד: כִּי עִמְּךָ הַסְּלִיחָה לְמַעַן תִּוָּרֵא: קִוִּיתִי יְיָ קִוְּתָה נַפְשִׁי וְלִדְבָרוֹ הוֹחָלְתִּי: נַפְשִׁי לַאדֹנָי מִשֹּׁמְרִים לַבֹּקֶר שֹׁמְרִים לַבֹּקֶר: יַחֵל יִשְׂרָאֵל אֶל יְיָ כִּי עִם יְיָ הַחֶסֶד וְהַרְבֵּה עִמּוֹ פְדוּת: וְהוּא יִפְדֶּה אֶת יִשְׂרָאֵל מִכֹּל עֲוֹנוֹתָיו:

**Shir** ha-ma-alot. Mi-ma-amakim k'ra-ticha Adonoi. Adonoi shima b'koli, ti-hi-yena aznecha kashuvot l'kol ta-cha-nunai. Im avonot tishmor Ya, Adonoi mi ya-amod. Ki imcha ha-slicha l'ma-an tivaray. Kiviti Adonoi kiv-ta nafshi v'lidvaro hochalti. Nafshi la-Adonoi mi-shomrim la-boker, shomrim la-boker. Yachel Yisrael el Adonoi ki im Adonoi ha-chesed v'harbeh imo f'dut. V'hu yif-deh et Yisrael mi-kol avonotav.

**A** *song of ascents. From the depths I call to You, God! God, listen to my voice; may Your ears be attuned to the sound of my pleas. If You would preserve sins, God, who could possibly withstand it? But forgiveness is Yours, that we may revere You. I have hoped for You, God, my soul has hoped, and for Your word I have hoped. My soul is anticipating God just as those who watch for the dawn, are* *watching for dawn. May Israel always hope toward God, for with God is kindness, and He has much redemption. And He will redeem Israel from all its misdeeds.*

God, sometimes I remember to turn to You in tough times, and sometimes I forget that You're there. I turn into control mode and delude myself into thinking I need to manage everything on my own. What a mistake! You are there, just waiting for us to ask You for help. No matter how low I am, no matter what mistakes I've made, You're there. You care. You forgive, You help, and You are kind. May I always remember Your presence and love when I am in need.

MAY I ALWAYS REMEMBER YOUR PRESENCE AND LOVE WHEN I AM IN NEED.

# Conclusion

# When God Says No

Whenever I finish praying, I feel cleansed. Although I've seen in my as-yet short sojourn on this planet that not all my prayers are "answered," I still appreciate what prayer can do in my life. Judaism teaches that the very process of prayer — no matter what the outcome — is a self-reflective activity that clarifies for ourselves what our needs and perspectives are. In fact, the Hebrew term for "to pray" is *"l'hitpallel"* — which literally means "to self-reflect."

But the inevitable question arises: what happens when I pray for something and it doesn't happen? Is God listening? Does prayer "work" or doesn't it?

The answer to this question is much longer than these lines, yet I feel compelled to address it, at least cursorily, here. I encourage you to do your own study of the question, but consider this an invitation to learn more.

God's answer to our prayers may take various forms. Sometimes, God says, "Yes! I was just waiting for you to ask!"

Sometimes, God's answer is, "No, this is not a good time for you to have that" or, "Not yet." God gives us what is good for us, and sometimes we ourselves aren't aware of what is good for us. As the adage goes, be careful what you pray for — you may get it. Sometimes, God's response is, "I have something even better in store for you," or, remarkably, "I am saving your prayer for the future." Prayer is like energy. It is never lost, only redirected or converted into a new form.

When we pray for someone else, there's another dynamic at play. When God sees that we are praying for another, He sees that our relationship with that person has awoken a spiritual piece of our hearts. That merit becomes conferred not just to us, but to the person we are praying for as well, since he or she was the catalyst for our spiritual response. God notes that merit as "belonging" to that person, and they receive spiritual benefit.

One thing is for certain: prayer always works. We just are not privy to the master plan. We don't know where it's working, for whom it's working, or in which generation it will take root.

By praying, we never lose. We connect to our source, to ourselves, and always, to God.

May this book assist you and inspire you in your journey.

# Appendix

# Recommended Reading

***This book is abridged; what can I try that is a complete, non-abridged prayerbook for year-round prayers?***

Scherman, Nosson. *The Complete Artscroll Siddur* (New York: Mesorah Publications, 1984).

This is the most complete translated prayerbook in modern times. It transformed my life as a child when I discovered a newly published copy and I remember asking my parents for my very own for a birthday present. I bought a new one as a high school graduate and took it with me to Israel, using it for every imaginable occasion till it was bedraggled. Fortunately, my fiancée bought me a leather-bound edition in honor of our forthcoming wedding. I still have it, though now, twenty-one years later, it has missing pages and a rebound spine. This book contains all the prayers, a beautiful overview on prayer, a very grammatically faithful translation (without "thee"s and "thou"s) based on multiple textual sources, and an anthologized commentary running along the bottom. It also contains prayers not usually found in your typical Siddur, such as special blessings for unusual events and prayers for death and bereavement.

***I want to become inspired in the concept of prayer. What are some non-prayerbook books that cover themes and inspiration about prayer?***

Kleinman, Heshy. *Praying with Fire* (New York: Mesorah Publications, 2005).

This book offers attitudes and approaches to prayer, inspiration, thematic concepts, and philosophical ideas. It's arranged for daily study, in a five-minute-a-day format. This is not a book to be read all at once, but rather to be studied a bit at a time for maximal long-term erudition and inspiration.

Nissel, Menachem. *Rigshei Lev* (Jerusalem: Targum Press, 2001).

The author himself gave this book to me as a gift. He is a family friend and an accomplished educator. It's a thematic and halachic (pertaining to Jewish law) discussion about women and prayer. It offers both practical guidance and spiritual inspiration, and is the only book of its kind that I'm aware of that focuses specifically on the relationship between women and prayer.

### What are other translations that I might find useful?

Twerski, Abraham J. *Prayerfully Yours* (New York: Mesorah Publications, 2001).

Twerski, Abraham J. *Twerski on Prayer* (New York: K'hal Publishing, 2004).

Note: these are the same book. The former is the coffee-table sized edition and the latter is a smaller, portable version.

While Rabbi Dr. Twerski has an incredible roster of Jewish self-development books to his name, this book is in a class all its own. It contains inspiration, translations, stories and explanations of selected prayers, and customs. It's beautifully laid out and even more beautifully expressed.

Kirzner, Yitzchok and Lisa Aiken. *The Art of Jewish Prayer* (Northvale: Jason Aronson, 1991).

A heartfelt exposition on the soul of prayer as based on its centerpiece, the Amidah prayer (otherwise known as *Shemoneh Esrei*). By delving deeply into each of the nineteen blessings of the prayer, the authors draw out basic themes in prayer that are sure to touch the hearts of the readers.

***I'm not such a "prayerbook" person. I find myself much more connected by talking to God my own way. Is there guidance on this?***

Kaplan, Aryeh. *Jewish Meditation* (New York: Schoken Books, 1985).

Rabbi Kaplan was a legendary person. He died young, with quite a legacy behind him. He was a renowned physicist and a modern-day kabbalist. His seminal work, *If You Were God*, literally changed my life when I found it at my grandparents' home on a visit. His slim volumes on the deepest concepts in mystical Judaism are mind-altering. In this work he delves into the non-traditional (but actually very traditional) state of mind that one should aim for in prayer, and how, specifically, to aim for it — whether that prayer is formal or informal. This book is to be handled with care. Quite honestly, there is much about it I don't understand. It is nevertheless useful for those who need to understand that these ideas are Jewish, and not solely the domain of other faiths.

Arush, Shalom. *In Forest Fields* (Jerusalem, 2009).

The ancient Jewish concept of "*hitbodedut*," or spiritual solitude, is the main factor discussed in this book. It discusses personal, non-scripted prayer, covering the when, where, why, and how. Many people who participate in regular communal prayer have never been introduced to the ideas in the book. Communal prayer is a starting point (just like organized religion is a starting point) — but true connection to God is the true goal.

***I feel so confused at synagogue. What's going on? Are there any books that can teach me?***

Donin, Hayim H. *To Pray as a Jew* (New York: Basic Books, 1991).

This is your comprehensive guide to synagogue doings. It covers the "why" and "how" technicalities of synagogue prayer, and also includes a guide to the Siddur with ethical and inspirational reminders of the big picture of prayer. It even includes a selection of prayers in both Hebrew and English with a detailed commentary. This is an indispensable guide for those who want to understand the formal practicalities of synagogue life.

## About The Author

Mrs. Ruchi Koval is the co-founder and director of the Jewish Family Experience, a family education center and Sunday school located in Cleveland, Ohio. She is the mother to seven children, is a certified parenting coach, runs Jewish character-development groups for women, and is a motivational speaker and blogger.

## About Mosaica Press

Mosaica Press is an independent publisher of Jewish books. Our authors include some of the most profound, interesting, and entertaining thinkers and writers in the Jewish community today. There is a great demand for high-quality Jewish works dealing with issues of the day — and Mosaica Press is helping fill that need. Our books are available around the world. Please visit us at **www.mosaicapress.com** or contact us at **info@mosaicapress.com**. We will be glad to hear from you.

MOSAICA PRESS

# About The Cover

The color blue represents meditation, and the strong tones convey the strength and power of prayer. The streaks of color are defined by a border, keeping it within the traditional framework, while pushing outside the boundary for something revolutionary and unexpected. Similarly, the fonts vacillate between modern and formal, as both components are crucial for prayerful expression.

Credit for cover design to Allyson Goldstein and Robin Green.

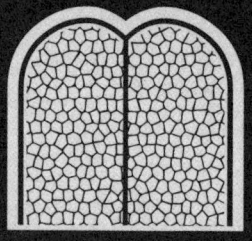

MOSAICA PRESS
BOOK PUBLISHERS
*Elegant, Meaningful & Bold*

info@MosaicaPress.com
www.MosaicaPress.com

The Mosaica Press team of acclaimed editors and designers is attracting some of the most compelling thinkers and teachers in the Jewish community today. Our books are available around the world.

HARAV YAACOV HABER
RABBI DORON KORNBLUTH